"Audra gives you the 'process' you need to let go of the past, create a new vision for your future, and develop a new self-image as God sees you. As a teacher and mentor of God's purpose, Audra's book will inspire you to reach for the plan God has for your life. If you truly want to find change for a better life, this book is for you."

BRENDA HOGAN
First Lady | Spring First Church, Spring, TX

"Audra Price is a woman full of the Holy Spirit, and has served and mentored women for many years. She is a gifted teacher, dynamic public speaker and author. Audra ministers with genuine compassion, and a deep desire to see women touched with the love and grace of God. She is a woman full of the wisdom of God and her life exemplifies truth, integrity and spiritual purity, which are qualities that speak highly of her personal core values. I highly recommend Audra Price to anyone without reservation."

LAURA GAGNON
Author | Teacher | Speaker

"I have known Audra Price for over ten years as a friend, and in the field of health and wellness. She is a godly woman that seeks God's counsel regarding any decision she makes. She is a wife, mother, wellness educator, gifted speaker, teacher, and author. Audra just exudes God's grace and I highly recommend getting to "know" her through her writing. She consciously chooses Jesus first and lives what she says!"

PAULA J. KRUPPSTADT, MD, FAAP, IFMCP
Fellow & Diplomate | American Academy of Pediatrics

"When I think of Audra Price, I think of a beautiful, graceful, attentive, caring faithful friend, and a woman of spiritual wisdom. Whatever Audra touches, she does with excellence and with the goal to serve the Lord through her service to others. These qualities are reflected in her life as a mother, wife, and as a business owner caring for others."

SONJA I. STAINES
Director | Excelsior School of Dance

"Audra Price is a mighty voice in the body of Christ. Her professional ethics and character as a leader, wife and mother are impeccable and highly sought after. She is a gifted writer and speaker, and I am truly honored to be associated with such a bright light in God's Kingdom."

ANNIE VARUGHESE MD, FACC
Medical Director & CEO
Advanced Cardiovascular Care Center

"It's been my pleasure to personally observe the amazing spirit-filled life of Audra. She consistently upholds her deep beliefs and convictions. She leads and mentors with a heart of love and God's truth. She nurtures her children with warmth and kindness and is a role model as a loving wife."

PAT WILLIAMS
Former Director | North Houston Section Women's Ministries

the process

FINDING GOD & YOUR PURPOSE IN THE MIDST OF LIFE'S TRIALS

AUDRA PRICE

the process

**FINDING GOD & YOUR PURPOSE
IN THE MIDST OF LIFE'S TRIALS**

BY AUDRA PRICE

Copyright © 2017 Audra Price. All rights reserved. Except for brief quotations for review purposes, no part of this book may be reproduced in any form without prior written permission from the author.

Published by:

LIFEWISE BOOKS
PO BOX 1072
Pinehurst, TX 77362
LifeWiseBooks.com

Cover Design and Interior Layout and Design | Yvonne Parks | PearCreative.ca

To contact the author:
www.AudraPrice.com

ISBN (Print): 978-1-947279-26-1
ISBN (Ebook): 978-1-947279-27-8

dedication

This Book is dedicated to my first love—Jesus Christ.
All things are possible with God to them that believe.

I also dedicate this book to my husband Daryl.
You are my best friend and prayer partner. Thank you for believing in me.

SPECIAL THANKS

To our five children: Jeremiah, Ketúrah, Noémi, Ethan, and Olivia. You have been gracious, loving and patient with me as God has taken me through many tough processes of life.

To our parents: Rev. Daryl Price, Sr. and Rose Price, and Rev. Lawrence C. and Betty Z. Collier, for raising us in godly homes.

To my dear friend, Margaret Zirkle, for investing time into this project with me.

table of contents

Foreword	7
Introduction	9
Chapter 1: Purpose for The Process	15
Chapter 2: The Process Takes Time	35
Chapter 3: God's View	53
Chapter 4: Unmask	77
Chapter 5: Wounds	91
Chapter 6: Issues	107
Chapter 7: Unseen War	119
Chapter 8: Strongholds	131
Chapter 9: Victim or Victor	155
Chapter 10: God's Salvation Process	169
Conclusion	183
About the Author	195
Endnotes	197
Works Cited	213

foreword

Finding God in the midst of life's tragedies and trials began my senior year in high school. I laid in agony on the ground awaiting the ambulance and transport to the emergency room. In my effort to assist our team's endeavors to advance to a championship, I miscalculated the distance to the first hurdle resulting in catastrophe.

As the cold rain continued to fall, my pain and grimace was abruptly replaced with laughter. The pain was unbearable, so why was I laughing? I overheard the EMS team commenting, "He's going into shock." The injuries were devastating.

I tore all but one ligament in my knee along with the nerve responsible for controlling foot and leg movement. The resulting muscular damage challenged and frustrated the orthopedic surgeon's plan for repair. After two surgeries lasting twelve and nine hours respectively, the Dr. sighed and said, "Well, we were able to repair 80% of the damage. It will take some time and you will walk with a limp, but eventually walk you will." This news was especially heartbreaking because only a few months prior, I had accepted a full scholarship to participate in Division I football.

Due to the severity of the injuries, I was required to lay mostly still for months which caused my body to atrophy to a shell of its former stature. How could God allow such tragedy at the culmination of my efforts? Though my mother tended to be quite stoic, I could only imagine her hurt and sense of hopelessness to see her son burdened with such pain and disappointment.

I have experienced the beauty and pain of the process firsthand. Whether you are at the beginning or feel you are at the end of your process, know God has a purpose and be ready for it to take more time than originally considered. To truly heal from the wounds incurred whether self-inflicted or at the hands of others, you must unmask and allow yourself to align your perspective with God's view of your situation.

The opening story, abridged as it seems, exemplifies a process where God ultimately accomplished His work "in spite of" versus "because of." This process culminated five years later with marriage to my lovely bride and a fourth-round draft selection in the NFL. God honored my small level of faith, and strengthened my resolve through a process initiated by calamity.

It was in my personal process that I found Audra, my best friend and my bride whom I have come to realize believes more in me than I do. That belief and encouragement continues to help me through my journey.

As you read *The Process*, Audra will share how to identify the issues holding you back, their possible sources, and provide insight into the unseen war for your attention, your family, and your identity. By the end, you will feel confident in your ability to recognize and approach the seen and unseen strongholds around you and establish victory over your situation.

Now let's begin this journey and see what God has to reveal concerning your past, your now and your future through *The Process*.

Daryl Price, Jr.
Loving Husband

introduction

"'For I know the plans I have for you,' says the Lord. 'They are plans for good and not for disaster, to give you a future and a hope.'" [1]

God has a plan for your life. How many times have you heard this statement? As powerful as it sounds, it raises many questions. For some, that statement might seem unattainable, distant, and beyond reach. Others are provoked to curiosity, eager to learn more and inquisitive about what God could possibly have in mind for them. Yet there are others who do not think knowing God's plan is possible.

Whatever our response is to that statement, whether we believe it to be true or not, God does have a plan. He doesn't reveal it once we are born or find that perfect birthday to show us. No, He takes us through a timeline of events, one day at a time, one year at a time, drawing us closer to Him so we can see what He sees in us and for us. He is always moving; He is never stagnant. He reveals to us His plan for the process and creates the steps necessary to fulfill that plan while leading, guiding and directing us through many of our life's challenges and accomplishments.

In fact, God has already prepared the process that is right for you, because He knows you have great capacity to do and be all that you were created for. If you are looking, He will unfold the process right before your eyes, showing you that the impossible is possible with Him.

The 23rd Psalm, one of my favorites, describes God as a shepherd. A shepherd leads his flock, guiding and directing them. He leads them through many paths and to many fields for them to graze, rest, and mate, all the while watching over them and keeping them safe from harm. Let's read it together.

> "The Lord is my Shepherd [to feed, to guide and to shield me], I shall not want. He lets me lie down in green pastures; He leads me beside the still and quiet waters. He refreshes and restores my soul (life); He leads me in the paths of righteousness for His name's sake. Even though I walk through the [sunless] valley of the shadow of death, I fear no evil, for Thou are with me; Your rod [to protect] and Your staff [to guide], they comfort and console me. You prepare a table before me in the presence of my enemies. You have anointed and refreshed my head with oil; my cup overflows. Surely goodness and mercy and unfailing love shall follow me all the days of my life, and I shall dwell forever [throughout all my days] in the house and in the presence of the Lord."[2]

God has you in the process. He does not do anything without the process in mind because He sees the value in the completion of what is ahead. He understands how you were created, because He created you. He understands your purpose, your personality, your passions, and your past. Because He has a plan for your future He knows the promises He has already set before you. He will guide you down the right path and lead you to your purpose. It is God's desire to walk you through the process of life unharmed and prepared for your destiny.

As a shepherd leads his flock into unfamiliar territory, he knows safety is important. The rocks, thorns, deep holes in the ground and lurking predators are a constant threat to the flock. Yet, having traveled before them, this knowledge gives him wisdom to know how to navigate properly. Where he is leading them is better for them in many ways. Good food, clean water and rest are a must if they are going to continue to their destination.

Just like the shepherd, God leads us through unfamiliar territory, watching over us and keeping us safe from unseen dangers. His word is a field to graze on. It fills the streams with fresh water daily and provides us with peace so we can rest. The word "through" means, "in at one end and out at the other."[3] God will not leave you alone when the hard places present themselves. He is committed to walking with you through life's twist and turns.

> "When you go through deep waters, I will be with you.
> When you go through rivers of difficulty, you will not drown.
> When you walk through the fire of oppression, you will not be burned up; the flames will not consume you."[4]

God will bring you in, "through," and out of the process, no matter how hard it is or how long it takes. His goal is to pace you for the duration of the process until you reach the end. He said He would never leave or abandon us. "Do not be afraid or discouraged, for the LORD will personally go ahead of you. He will be with you; He will neither fail you nor abandon you."[5]

> "Even though I walk through the [sunless] valley of the shadow of death, I fear no evil, for You are with me; Your rod [to protect] and Your staff [to guide], they comfort and console me."

Don't fear the "shadow of death." It is only a shadow. Shadows form around objects, then magnify them exponentially. You can't see the shadow without the presence of light. So, when you see it, know that light is right there. Jesus is the light of the world. He does not want you to fear. His rod and staff are there to protect and guide you, even though the enemy might be present.

Don't be afraid or discouraged when you aren't as far along in the process as you want to be. He has already moved ahead of you preparing the way, which means He knows the terrain of the land and where there are peaks and valleys. Imagine God placing His prints in the ground for you to follow. Imagine each step planned perfectly. All you have to do is follow behind and let Him be your guide. Your steps are ordered of the Lord.

> "The steps of a good man are ordered by the Lord, and He delights in his way. Though he fall, he shall not be utterly cast down; for the Lord upholds him with His hand."[6]

Notice the phrase, "Though he (she) fall." During the process, you may fall because you can't see the prints. It is not uncommon for hikers to fall on the trail because they are thrown off by the condition of the path. They often fall because they are unfamiliar with the environment. They look around, up and down, and misplace their step. You may fall because you are not familiar with where you are—but God will hold you with "His hand."

introduction

It is also normal to question the process, but God has a way of comforting and encouraging us to keep walking. When you are about to take your last few steps, your mind may be flooded with worry that you didn't get to the right place. God has a destination for the process, and it is His responsibility to get you there.

Take the last few minutes of a baby being born. The last few contractions are the hardest and become increasingly intense and more frequent, because they are forcing the baby to make its final descent down the birth canal. This is the time when I wanted to give up for sure, when my own children were being born. The pain and pressure was unbearable, even though the baby was almost out. This would be the worst place for the baby to get stuck.

They are under the most stress, with their heads squeezed in the tight space, their faces smashed against the bones, and shoulders tight with nowhere to move. The baby monitor indicates the stress level has increased the baby's heart rate. But then the head comes out, leading the way for the rest of the body. The new life is now ready to meet Mom and Dad. It is worth it to stay in the press of the process.

Ultimately, the process stretches throughout your entire life, revealing who you are. It produces healing physically, spiritually, and emotionally, transforming you into who God wrote about in the books of heaven, a person made in God's image and likeness.[7]

God wants to guide you through life, not just in one way but in every way; not just at one time but every time; and not just in one situation, but all situations. These plans are good, morally excellent, virtuous, righteous, and of high quality. They are for your future. With every plan, every path and every process your purpose is revealed. Finally, through the process, God gives us hope.

Process is a "systematic series of actions directed to some end. A continuous action, operation, or series of changes taking place in a definite manner."[8] It is important to understand that the process is the beginning of something new and fresh. Continue on the path until the end. Walk with expectancy because along the path are many souvenirs to pick up and share with others. Once you have settled into the fact that you are in the process with God, it will be easier to move towards your future with great hope, knowing that God will see you through. Knowing that He has so perfectly prepared you for your purpose, trusting seems to come naturally. Trust the process because God has a plan for your life!

CHAPTER 1
purpose for the process

"My brethren, count it all joy when you fall into various trials, knowing that the testing of your faith produces patience. But let patience have its perfect work, that you may be perfect and complete, lacking nothing. If any of you lacks wisdom, let him ask of God, who gives to all liberally and without reproach, and it will be given to him..." [1]

The process is a progressive series of events that directs us towards arrival at a specific and predetermined destination. God's intended outcome of any process in our lives is to refine and produce revelation in relation to our life's purpose. Revelation is "an act of revealing or communicating divine truth" and something that is revealed by God to people.[2]

Knowledge is "the fact or condition of knowing something with familiarity gained through experience or association: the fact or condition of being aware of something: the range of one's information or understanding answered to the best of my knowledge: the circumstance or condition of apprehending truth or fact through reasoning: the fact or condition of having information or of being learned a person of unusual knowledge."[3]

Revelation knowledge is revealed information and understanding given by God to help bring what is hidden and in secret to light. "The secret things belong to the Lord our God, but those things which are revealed belong to us and to our children forever, that we may do all the words of this law."[4]

I believe God is the revealer of truth and that He reveals truth to us for many reasons such as:

1. To set us free: "You will know the truth and the truth will set you free."[5]
2. To make us aware of His activity on earth: "Surely the Lord God does nothing, unless He reveals His secret to His servants the prophets."[6]
3. To reveal the sin in our lives: "Now He who searches the hearts knows what the mind of the Spirit is, because He makes intercession for the saints according to the will of God."[7]

Now, I would like to discuss what God reveals to us about the word "trial" used in James 1:2. A trial is the process by which God uses to reveal certain aspects about us or our current circumstances. A trial can be good or bad depending on the issue. A trial is "the act of trying, testing, or putting to the proof. An attempt or effort to do something. A tentative or experimental action in order to ascertain results; experiment."[8] The legal definition for "trial" is "the determination of a person's guilt or innocence by due process of law."[9] Here are some key points and scriptures about trials that June

Hunt from "Hope for the Heart" wrote in her article, "Trials."[10]

Trials are experienced by everyone

"Dear friends, don't be surprised at the fiery trials you are going through, as if something strange were happening to you."[1]

Trials have a divine purpose

"We can rejoice, too, when we run into problems and trials, for we know that they help us develop endurance. And endurance develops strength of character, and character strengthens our confident hope of salvation. And this hope will not lead to disappointment. For we know how dearly God loves us, because he has given us the Holy Spirit to fill our hearts with his love."[12]

Trials last only for a while

"So be truly glad. There is wonderful joy ahead, even though you must endure many trials for a little while."[13]

Trials are controlled by God

"The temptations in your life are no different from what others experience. And God is faithful. He will not allow the temptation to be more than you can stand. When you are tempted, He will show you a way out so that you can endure."[14]

Trials strengthen you in your weakness

"That is why, for Christ's sake, I delight in weaknesses, in insults, in hardships, in persecutions, in difficulties. For when I am weak, then I am strong."[15]

Trials come with God's grace for endurance

> "Each time he said, "My grace is all you need. My power works best in weakness." So now I am glad to boast about my weaknesses, so that the power of Christ can work through me."[16]

Notice the words "due process" in the legal definition of "trial" provided above. A trial has a process. The "process of law" is often referred to as the due process of law, due process, due course of law. It is defined as the regular administration of the law, according to which no citizen may be denied his or her legal rights and all laws must conform to fundamental, accepted legal principles, as the right of the accused to confront his or her accusers. "The origin of this term 'due process' originated in 1215 A.D. with the English Magna Carta, an important provision of which was that no freeman would be deprived of certain rights except 'by the judgment of his peers and by the law of the land.'"[17]

Dann McCreary, has a great explanation of "The Elements of Biblical Due Process," in his article, "Biblical Due Process: God's Specification for Earthly Justice." Dann gives seven elements of biblical due process and supporting scriptures. These elements help to give us a better understanding of "due process" in context of how sin broke the law of God and that it's penalty was death.

> <u>The Law</u> – In order for a crime to take place, there must first be a law. The law sets forth some requirement for behavior. Adam and Eve were charged and penalized only because God had previously said to them 'Thou shalt not.'
>
> But of the tree of the knowledge of good and evil, thou

shalt not eat of it: for in the day that thou eatest thereof thou shalt surely die.[18]

<u>A Violation of the Law</u> – After there is an established law in place, a violation of that law must occur. Some person, to whom the law applies, must transgress that law.

And when they had threatened them further, they let them go (finding no basis on which they might punish them).[19] Obviously, if no one violates the law, there is no problem and no further need for due process.

<u>Witnesses</u> – In order to establish the fact of a transgression of the law, there must be at least two witnesses to the violation of that law:

One witness shall not rise up against a man for any iniquity, or for any sin, in any sin that he sinneth: at the mouth of two witnesses, or at the mouth of three witnesses, shall the matter be established.[20]

<u>The Charge</u> – There must be an accusation made by the witnesses. In civil society, this accusation is known as an indictment. "The definition of an indictment is a charge or formal written accusation charging someone with a crime."[21]

"Pilate asked for an indictment when Jesus was led before him in the Praetorium: Pilate therefore went out to them, and said, 'What accusation do you bring against this Man?'"[22]

<u>The Tribunal</u> – There must be a judicial body qualified to pass judgement. In civil society, this is the civil magistrate

and the courts of law, and is known as a 'court of competent jurisdiction.' In the church, this is usually the governing body of elders, but ultimately, when a transgression is not repented of, it is the whole congregation who passes judgement.[23]

<u>The Sentence</u> – There must be a just sentence imposed by a duly authorized judge. When the Jews did not have the requisite authority to put Jesus to death, they brought Him before someone who did.

'Then said Pilate unto them, 'Take ye him, and judge him according to your law.' The Jews therefore said unto him, 'It is not lawful for us to put any man to death.'"[24]

<u>The Penalty</u> – Finally, the penalty of the sentence must be carried out.

'For the wages of sin is death.'[25]

It should be clear that the process can and should be terminated at any of several points if God's requirements for proceeding are not met. Why is due process important? It is mandatory that those wielding authority adhere to God's standard of justice by acting in accord with these enumerated principles of Biblical due process. Scripture repeatedly emphasizes the obligation of just judgement laid upon those who rule."[26]

Did you notice that each stage of the Biblical Due Process has a purpose? The purpose for this process is to make sure there is justice. God is a just and righteous God. He wants to make sure that we understand His perfect plan for our lives is to be with Him eternally. Once the "law" was broken by Adam and Eve in the garden of Eden, there needed to be a way for God to be just, as well as, the need for mankind not receive the just penalty of death. "The wages of sin is death, but the gift of God is eternal life in Christ Jesus our Lord."[27]

Yes, the law that was broken by Adam and Eve was considered sin. Adam and Eve were on trial and grace was extended to them by God. Since death was the penalty, a life was given in place of theirs. A lamb was sacrificed for them. This lamb represents Jesus, and He chooses to be the sacrifice for us. We broke the law through our sin, but Jesus gave His life so we can live in Him.

As we read this scripture again, let's look at the word "trial" thru the eyes of revelation. Consider the trials of your life as a process by which God uses to get you into closer alignment with Him. When we summarize James 1:2, understanding that trials are simply a process, certain clarities are revealed.

>*The process* produces joy.
>*The process* gives revelation knowledge.
>*The process gives* certain truths about the person and the situation.
>*The process* tests our faith.
>*The process* produces patience.
>*The process* helps us work towards perfection and completeness in God.
>*The process* helps us to search for wisdom.
>*The process* opens doors for communication with God.
>*The process* brings stability to our situation.
>*The process* strengthens our faith.

A trial is the act of trying and testing. When we think about a trial we often see it as negative. The thought of a case gone wrong or someone being sentenced to life in prison presents a level of uncertainty. Or we think of justice for those who were systematically oppressed or victimized. Most people do not enjoy taking tests or the thought of ever having to be on trial. We know at the end there is either going to be justice or injustice, depending on our perception.

We must see that a trial can simply be "the process" in which God is using to bring us into a deeper relationship with Him. God wants to reveal who He is in the midst of the process so He can heal you and begin the transformation process in you. One scripture I pray over myself and my family each day is Ephesians 1:17-18. "I keep asking that the God of our Lord Jesus Christ, the glorious Father, may give you the spirit of wisdom and revelation, so that you may know Him better. I pray that the eyes of your heart may be enlightened in order that you may know the hope to which He has called you, the riches of His glorious inheritance in His holy people." I personally, want to understand what God is doing during the process so I can gain wisdom which is only going to help me in the future.

Within our text from James, there are many benefits gained from walking through the process. These benefits are souvenirs we pick up on the way. They are gold nuggets with great potential if we can see their true value: faith, joy, patience, wisdom and trust.

FAITH

Hebrews 11 begins with quite a bold statement about faith. "The fundamental fact of existence is that this trust in God, this faith, is the firm foundation under everything that makes life worth living. It's our handle on what we can't see. The act of faith is what distinguished our ancestors, set them above the crowd."[28]

Faith becomes part of the process when we cannot see our way around the new terrain of our circumstances. It is faith that pushes us towards Jesus, who is the way, the truth, and the life. Faith helps us gain peace about the issues of life that we cannot clearly understand because we cannot clearly see.

It is faith that reveals what already exists in us. It pushes us into the world of the unseen to apprehend truth and brings it into existence in the natural and the now. It is this very faith that the writer of Hebrews praises by celebrating the great patriarchs and matriarchs of the Bible. "Through their faith, the people in days of old earned a good reputation. By faith we understand that the entire universe was formed at God's command, that what we now see did not come from anything that can be seen."[29]

This test of faith in the process is to help us to see what isn't seen so we can be drawn toward God's plan for our lives. Let's read some accounts of faith:

> "It was by faith that Abel brought a more acceptable offering to God than Cain did. Abel's offering gave evidence that he was a righteous man, and God showed His approval of his gifts. Although Abel is long dead, he still speaks to us by his example of faith.
>
> It was by faith that Enoch was taken up to heaven without dying: 'he disappeared, because God took him.' For before he was taken up, he was known as a person who pleased God. And it is impossible to please God without faith. Anyone who wants to come to Him must believe that God exists and that He rewards those who sincerely seek Him.

the process

It was by faith that Noah built a large boat to save his family from the flood. He obeyed God, who warned him about things that had never happened before. By his faith Noah condemned the rest of the world, and he received the righteousness that comes by faith.

It was by faith that Abraham obeyed when God called him to leave home and go to another land that God would give him as his inheritance. He went without knowing where he was going. And even when he reached the land God promised him, he lived there by faith—for he was like a foreigner, living in tents. And so did Isaac and Jacob, who inherited the same promise. Abraham was confidently looking forward to a city with eternal foundations, a city designed and built by God.

It was by faith that even Sarah was able to have a child, though she was barren and was too old. She believed that God would keep His promise. And so a whole nation came from this one man who was as good as dead—a nation with so many people that, like the stars in the sky and the sand on the seashore, there is no way to count them.

All these people died still believing what God had promised them. They did not receive what was promised, but they saw it all from a distance and welcomed it. They agreed that they were foreigners and nomads here on earth. Obviously, people who say such things are looking forward to a country they can call their own. If they had longed for the country they came from, they could have gone back. But they were looking for a better place, a heavenly homeland. That is why God is not ashamed to be called their God, for He has prepared a city for them."[30]

Now let's jump to verse 32:

"How much more do I need to say? It would take too long to recount the stories of the faith of Gideon, Barak, Samson, Jephthah, David, Samuel, and all the prophets. By faith these people overthrew kingdoms, ruled with justice, and received what God had promised them. They shut the mouths of lions, quenched the flames of fire, and escaped death by the edge of the sword. Their weakness was turned to strength. They became strong in battle and put whole armies to flight. Women received their loved ones back again from death."[31]

It does not surprise me that whenever I find myself in the process, my faith rises to a new level. I found this to be true every time I gave birth to a new baby. My husband and I have five children. Each of the five pregnancies was completely different. If I am totally honest, I would have to admit, I never enjoyed being pregnant. Yes, I was amazed that a new life could grow in my womb. I was also excited to know their sex, see their heartbeat, feel them move, and watch them develop and grow. But the prolonged sickness, nausea, swelling, and sleepless nights were all I could think about at the time.

Our first baby came six weeks early. I was not prepared for this in any way. I didn't have the nursery finished or even a bassinet for our son to sleep in when we brought him home. He took us all by surprise. The doctor said, "Audra, your water broke and you need to go to the hospital!" I just looked at her, crying and said, "Now?" She said, ever so calmly, "Yes. Why are you crying? The baby is going to be fine—he is just a little early."

My heart was full of fear because all I could think about at the time was the pain, getting an epidural and wondering if our baby was going to be ok. As I waddled slowly to my car, I said a silent prayer, "Lord, help me." This was a faith moment for me, for sure. Many times, my faith had been tested, but never had a test produced so much pain. After six hours of faith-testing labor, our first baby was born, five pounds, four ounces and perfect.

JOY

There was joy every time we held our son in our arms. Although I clearly remembered the pain, it was worth it because I received the promise, our baby. There is joy in knowing the process will have a great impact on your life. There will be pain and discomfort. James encourages us to seek joy when we recognize we are in the process because we will need it along the way. The joy of the Lord gives us strength to climb to the next level of our faith.[32] We know there will be times when the climb is hard and sadness comes our way but God has given us the oil of joy to keep are spirits up.

Joy is a part of the fruit of the Holy Spirit, as taught in Galatians 5:22-23: "But the Holy Spirit produces this kind of fruit in our lives: love, joy, peace, patience, kindness, goodness, faithfulness, gentleness, and self-control. There is no law against these things!" The Holy Spirit gives us what we need to live a life full of joy. The fruit are essential attributes that should be found in the life of a Christian. Have you ever meet a person who never seems to get down? They are genuinely happy most of the time. This is because the fruit of joy is something they actually live.

PATIENCE

Patience is another part of the fruit of the Holy Spirit. While most of us would like to always feel joyful, being patient is a whole different story. "Be patient." The last words any child wants to hear from his parent is to "be patient." The child kicks and screams as if what they are waiting for will never come. This is not far from the way we as children of God behave. It is as if patience makes all movement stop. Just hearing the word "patience" makes us roll our eyes and sigh because it makes the wait even longer. We want what we want, when we want it.

James 1:4 instructs, "But let patience have its perfect work, that you may be perfect and complete, lacking nothing." The first thing to note is that patience, in this context, is ongoing. It is at work continually. It is active and not passive. The process of patience will produce sustainable, concrete change, if we persevere. Secondly, the Greek work for perfect is "teleios or telos." Here perfect means "reaching an end or complete in all its parts, specifically of the completeness of Christian character. Mature (consummated) from going through the necessary stages to reach the end-goal, i.e. developed into a consummating completion by fulfilling the necessary process (spiritual journey)." [33]

Finally, patience lacks nothing good or important. Patience does not cause us to miss out, but rather to enjoy what we are waiting for even more. It takes time to get the cake baked.

WISDOM

The process helps us search for wisdom. Wisdom is "the quality or state of being wise; knowledge of what is true or right coupled with just judgment as to action; sagacity, discernment, or insight."[34]

Remember I said earlier that we need to understand what God is doing during the process to gain wisdom? Well, wisdom is what gives us insight and insight can increase faith. The process reveals the need for character growth in our lives. There are many scriptures in the Bible about wisdom. I was told years ago to read a chapter from the book of Proverbs each day. I find that it keeps me focused on making good clear decisions:

> "Wisdom is the principal thing; therefore, get wisdom and with all thy getting get understanding."[35]

> "The fear of the Lord is the beginning of wisdom and the knowledge of the Holy One is understanding."[36]

Wisdom is so important that God gave an immense amount to King Solomon simply because he asked for it. It pleases God for us to ask and search for wisdom. When is the last time you found yourself in a process and you stopped and asked God for wisdom? Asking for wisdom is like asking for directions when we are lost. If we ask, we will get to the destination faster. If we do not ask, it will take more time and there will be an increase of frustration.

Wisdom should be one of the first things we ask for. Seeking it is a true sign of maturity. It should be the treasure we are looking for. It is normal to find ourselves in difficult or different situations that cause us to question where we are in life. Without wisdom, it is impossible to know what to do during these times. Try to stop complaining when you don't understand something. Ask God for wisdom and listen for instruction.

TRUST

The process requires trust in God: "Trust in the Lord with all your heart and lean not on your own understanding; in all your ways acknowledge Him, and He shall direct your paths."[37] It isn't easy to trust what we don't understand. Nor is it easy to trust someone to lead us to a place that is unfamiliar. That is why we need to trust God, He is our shepherd. So, why do we need to trust God with all our hearts? The heart is where our actions flow from. We tend to follow our hearts, which can lead us astray or in the wrong direction.

The heart isn't the most reliable source of direction nor can it give us wisdom. The Bible encourages us to guard and keep our hearts pure because out of the heart is the "wellspring of life," Proverbs 4:23. Our hearts need to be pure so we can have clear understanding and not be led by our emotions. When we acknowledge God, He leads and directs us down the right path. We must trust God.

The purpose for the process is to move us from one place in life to the next. Revelation knowledge allows to us see what is hidden so we don't trip and fall. The process happens in stages. Faith, joy, patience, wisdom, and trust are stages in the process. Faith to produce action, joy to endure the journey, patience to finish, wisdom to understand where we are going and trust to want to know God's plan.

VALUE OF THE PROCESS

When I think about the value of something, I think about its worth and importance. I also wonder what makes it so valuable. In recent years, economists have promoted gold as a precious commodity that would be easily tradable if something were to happen to our currency. Gold isn't valued in the ground, or even once extracted from the earth. It isn't valued until it has gone through a refining process.

> "But who can endure the day of His coming?
> And who can stand when He appears?
> For He is like a refiner's fire
> And like launderer's soap.
> He will sit as a refiner and a purifier of silver;
> He will purify the sons of Levi,
> And purge them as gold and silver,
> That they may offer to the Lord
> An offering in righteousness."[38]

This scripture calls God a "refiner's fire" who will purify the sons of Levi. Levi was the priestly tribe in Israel, whose sons were raised to serve in the Temple of God. These priests were to be consecrated and purified, purged as gold and silver. This was a symbol of how God would purify hearts and motives.

The process of refining can be a very hazardous. The mines need to be stabilized to ensure the miners are protected during the extraction of the underground rocks. This is a great way to understand how God wants to transform our character into the character of Christ. Although He knows the process can be painful, He takes extra care to provide stability to us through His name: "The name of the Lord is a strong tower."[39] There are six stages of the refining process for gold and silver:[40]

1. **Breaking of ore**
   Breaking the ore exposes the value of the metals. We need the chains of sin and bondage to be broken off of us. Jesus did that on the cross. "Is not my word like fire," declares the Lord, "and like a hammer that breaks a rock in pieces?"[41]

2. **Crushed ore is placed in a crucible**

   The crucible is a dish that can withstand the intense heat of the furnace so the metal can melt. God holds us in His hands like a crucible while we are in the furnace to test our hearts. This process brings purity to our hearts and allows us to develop the character of God. "The crucible for silver and the furnace for gold, but the Lord tests the heart."[42]

3. **Removal of the dross**

   The crucible is necessary to remove the dross. Dross represents the impurities found in the metal and thus the impurities found in our hearts. If the dross isn't removed, the metal will not ever become pure. Once it cools and hardens, the impure dross becomes a part of the rock again. "Remove the dross from the silver, and a silversmith can produce a vessel."[43]

4. **More heat**

   The heat is turned up seven times in the furnace to remove all the dross. Each time the refiner pulls the crucible out, skims off the dross, and then returns it back into the heat. Sometimes when we are hurting and the heat is turned up in our lives, we want God to take it away. But we do not understand that God is adding heat to continue to remove the impurities of sin and wrong thinking, the dross. "And the words of the Lord are flawless, like silver purified in a crucible, like gold refined seven times."[44]

5. **The purification process**
   As the dross is removed, the metal is purified, and it becomes more valuable. Our physical bodies have a natural purification process. Unwanted waste is expelled from the body to keep the blood and organs pure and functioning properly. Once the process is over, it is normal to have clarity of mind and more energy. "He knows the way that I take; when He has tested me, I will come forth as gold."[45]

6. **The image of the refiner**
   The process is complete when there is a reflection of the refiner in the metal. Remember, we were made in the image of God. Although the testing of our faith can be painful, God understands the need in our lives to reflect Him. We are called to be His witness throughout the earth. "So God created man in His own image; in the image of God He created him; male and female He created them."[46]

Throughout the refining process, God is more concerned with building our character than our comfort. He knows that the suffering is there. He is not ignoring it, but He is trying to redefine our focus. It is not our reflection or our glory He is trying to see, but His own reflection and image in and through us. "Beloved, do not think it strange concerning the fiery trial (the process) which is to try you, as though some strange thing happened to you; but rejoice to the extent that you partake of Christ's sufferings, that when His glory is revealed, you may also be glad with exceeding joy."[47]

ACTIVATION

Ask God to take you through the refining process. Find a quiet place and play worship music. Begin to pour your heart out to the Lord. Tell Him your cares and burdens. Confess your sins (ores). Tell God you give Him permission to take you through this process without any interruptions because you trust Him.

ACTIVATION PRAYER

Dear Abba, Your word says You are a refining fire and Your desire is to purify me so that I might offer a sacrifice of righteousness unto You.[48] "Is not my word like fire and like a hammer that breaks a rock in pieces?"[49] Take Your word, and break away the ore of my heart, mind, body and spirit. Place me in the crucible of Your hands, and put me in the furnace of Your word and love. Remove the dross in my speech, my actions, my heart, and my mind, and turn up the heat so I can become Your image and reflect Your goodness, mercy, love, joy, peace, patience, faithfulness, and self-control.[50] Lord, I want to come forth as pure gold. In Jesus' name, Amen.

CHAPTER 2
the process takes time

When I was little girl, my mom and dad bought my siblings and I an audio Bible storybook that had two 45-rpm records. It was a great gift because I loved to listen to music and dance. That Christmas, I also got my very first record player. It was red and blue and just the right size for me to carry it all around the house. My little sister and I would play the Bible storybook record and follow along with the colored pages for hours just listening to Bible stories. The stories helped the Bible to come alive in my mind. It began with the creation story, and included were colorful pictures of the heavens, the sea creatures, the animals, and of course Adam and Eve. This format was a great way for me to learn history through the Bible.

I love history—I guess you could say I'm somewhat of a "history buff," especially when it comes to understanding events in a timeline. I like to read and hear about events that were going on in different parts of the world at the same time. I like to visualize timelines in my mind, which help me stay on course. As a homeschool mother, my favorite subject to teach is history. The best history lessons came from *Mysteries of History*, by Linda Lacour Hobar.[1] This curriculum incorporated many timelines.

I'm always trying to keep the family organized. With each kid having different activities on different days—doctor's appointments, dentist appointments and church activities—it can be hard to know what's what. When you have a big family, you need to keep things in order, which is why I love calendars. Calendars help me keep our busy lives in order and organized. They give me a visual of where we have been, what is going on now, and where we are headed. The Bible is very much like a calendar or timeline. It tells us the past, present, and future.

As you are going through the process, it's very important that you understand that the process takes time. A great way to understand this is to see yourself on an imaginary timeline. I call it a historical and eternal timeline. If you start from your conception month and follow along to the point where you are right now, it allows you to see how much God is involved in getting you to the point where you are today. It is comforting to remember that God can walk you through life—one step, one day, and one year at a time.

Another way I like to look at the process is through the metaphor of human development, beginning with the process of conception, over the nine months of growth, and finally through delivery.[2]

CONCEPTION TO BIRTH

The Ovulation Process

"Between periods, women ovulate, releasing a mature egg

from one of the ovaries. Ovulation usually occurs about a week before (or after) a woman's period...[3]

The Fertilization Process
If "a sperm cell is alive in the fallopian tube, it's capable of fertilizing an egg. If there's no egg in the fallopian tube, there's no chance of fertilization...Once a sperm cell penetrates the exterior of the egg, fertilization occurs—its DNA payload is delivered as the sperm is absorbed by the egg."[4]

The Embryo Implantation Process
"The zygote then makes a four-day journey down the fallopian tube toward the uterus, aided again by the tiny hair-like structures lining the tube. After about five days, the zygote will have made its way into the uterus. In one more day, this mass of cells will "hatch" from its thin-walled sac."[5]

The Development and Growth Process
"The embryo continues to develop the heart, blood cells, brain and spine, facial features, all in a sack of fluid called the embryonic sac."[6]

These processes are vital. They are the foundation for growth and development of the fetus. Let's read the accounts of the month to month process explained by The Cleveland Clinic:[7]

Eight Weeks
"The embryonal is now called a fetus."

Third Month
"During the third month, the baby's finger, toes, legs, and arms grow. The vital organs are developed and functioning.

The most critical part of the baby's development is over, and the baby continues to grow."

Fourth Month
"The baby's heartbeat can be heard, and the reproductive organs and genitals are completely developed."

Fifth Month
"Activity begins because muscles are developed, and there is movement in the womb."

Sixth month
"The baby responds to sounds and might even get hiccups. Babies born during this time have a great chance of surviving and are considered premature. They need extra care."

Seventh month
"The baby will continue to mature and develop reserves of body fat. The baby's hearing is fully developed. The amniotic fluid begins to diminish."

Eighth Month
"The baby's brain is developing at a rapid pace, and the baby can see and hear. Most internal systems are well developed, but the lungs may still be immature."

Ninth Month
"The baby continues to grow and mature: the lungs are nearly fully developed. He or she can blink, close the eyes, turn the head, grasp firmly, and respond to sounds, light, and touch. The baby's position changes to prepare itself for labor and delivery."

The Labor Process
"Labor begins when the cervix begins to open (dilate) and

thin (called effacement). The muscles of the uterus tighten (contract) at regular intervals, causing the cervix to thin and open. During contractions, the abdomen becomes hard. Between contractions, the uterus relaxes, and the abdomen becomes soft."[8]

THE BIRTHING PROCESS

Labor is the process by which the fetus and the placenta leave the uterus. Delivery can occur in two ways, vaginally or by a cesarean delivery.

"Labor occurs in three stages and can begin weeks before a woman delivers her infant. The first stage begins with the woman's first contractions and continues until she is dilated fully (ten centimeters, or four inches), which means the cervix has stretched to prepare for birth. The second stage is the active stage, in which the pregnant woman begins to push downward. It begins with complete dilation of the cervix and ends with the actual birth. The third stage, or placental stage, begins with the birth and ends with the completed delivery of the placenta and afterbirth."[9]

Each stage of the process of life in the womb is necessary to produce life outside the womb. There would not be a baby birthed, if only a few of these stages took place. Six months is the time when the baby can safely live outside the womb. Any earlier the baby may not survive because they are still dependent on the mother's blood supply and nutrients for further development. Each process is to ensure the safety of the baby throughout its entire developmental process. Notice the "Conception Process." If we look again at what happens during conception we will see that this is where new life begins here on earth. The egg and sperm meet, the egg is fertilized, the embryo is planted in the uterus and the development begins.

Isn't it interesting that God said before we were in our mother's womb He knew us? "I knew you before I formed you in your mother's womb. Before you were born I set you apart and appointed you as my prophet to the nations."[10] How is it that God 'set apart and appointed" the prophet Jeremiah before he was in his mother's womb? I believe this question reveals the mystery behind the Lord's prayer found in Matthew 6:9-13.

> "After this manner therefore pray ye:
> Our Father which art in heaven, hallowed be thy name.
> Thy kingdom come, Thy will be done in earth, as it is in heaven.
> Give us this day our daily bread.
> And forgive us our debts, as we forgive our debtors.
> And lead us not into temptation, but deliver us from evil:
> For thine is the kingdom, and the power, and the glory, forever. Amen."

"Thy kingdom come, Thy will be done in earth, as it is in heaven." God knew Jeremiah in heaven and called him to the earth when it was time. God knew you in heaven and called you to the earth when it was time. God knew exactly where and when to place us on the earth's timeline. He knew everything about us. Our parents, ethnic background, location, likes and dislikes, etc. He knew all about us before we were here. God was already thinking about you when He formed the earth. He had a perfect plan for you to enter the world through your mother's womb at a specific time. You were not a mistake, regardless of the circumstances surrounding your conception. God set you in motion to be born, live in Him, and eventually be His witness on earth. Now that is powerful!

THE PROCESS OF TIME

Let's look at a story found in 1 Samuel 1-3 about a woman named Hannah who gave birth to a son named Samuel in "the process of time."

> "And he had two wives: the name of one was Hannah, and the name of the other Peninnah (pa-nina). Peninnah had children, but Hannah had no children."[11]

In those days, it was thought that a woman was cursed if she didn't have children. The rejection she felt from her husband and others was a burden too heavy to bare for some women. Being barren caused many challenges in the family. Children were heirs to the inheritance, worked to produce food for the family and were raised to protect the family's investments.

Many men had multiple wives for producing children. We see this type of family unit in Genesis 21 with Abraham, Sarah, his wife, and Hagar (Sarah's handmaid). There were times a wife would allow her maidservant to produce children for her with her husband, if she was unable to have children or if she had not delivered a son. The story of Hannah begins in 1 Samuel:

> "This man went up from his city yearly to worship and sacrifice to the LORD of hosts in Shiloh. Also, the two sons of Eli, Hophni and Phinehas, the priests of the LORD, were there. And whenever the time came for Elkanah to make an offering, he would give portions to Peninnah his wife and to all her sons and daughters. But to Hannah he would give

a double portion, for he loved Hannah, although the LORD had closed her womb."[12]

Peninnah was one of the wives of Elkanah, and she had given birth to many sons and daughters. Peninnah and her children were given a portion of the meat offering. But Hannah, whom Elkanah loved, was given a double portion, a choice portion or generous helping. Could it be that Elkanah wanted to make sure Hannah knew she had his attention and love, although she could not give him children? You might not always have what you want but God still wants you to know you are loved by Him. You have His attention.

"And her rival also provoked her severely, to make her miserable, because the LORD had closed her womb."[13] Peninnah was Hannah's rival. A rival can be "a person who is competing for the same object or goal as another, or who tries to equal or outdo another; competitor."[14] How many of you have ever had a rival? Rivals come in all stages of life and for many reasons. There can be rivals in sports, academics, families, and even church. The high school I attended was the smallest in our district, yet we outperformed most of the schools in academics and athletics for many consecutive years. We had many rivals who wanted to take us down. We were the school that everyone talked about.

In 1 Samuel 1:6, The Message version reads as follows: "But her rival wife taunted her cruelly, rubbing it in and never letting her forget that GOD had not given her children." Rivals provoke and taunt until they see signs of weakness. They like to get their opponent to the place where they cannot focus on goals or promises. In this story, Peninnah was working like Satan, who was prowling around like a roaring lion, seeking to devour someone, Hannah.[15]

Satan also accuses us before our God day and night.[16] He taunts us about our past as well as our present circumstance and will try to lie to us about the future to see if he can find a crack in our faith. Peninnah was no different, and neither is your rival. "So it was, year by year, when she went up to the house of the Lord, that she provoked her; therefore she wept and did not eat."[17]

Elkanah could see the distress and sadness of Hannah, so he asked her a series of questions in verse 8. The last one is what we will focus on: "Then Elkanah her husband said to her, 'Hannah, why do you weep? Why do you not eat? And why is your heart grieved? Am I not better to you than ten sons?'"[18]

"Am I not better to you than ten sons?" he asks her. With this question, he points out that their love for each other is a blessing. The process takes time, and sometimes our longing for something does not allow us to see the blessings all around us. There are times when we don't see that the blessings far outweigh the loss or longing in our hearts.

We can want something so badly that God has to check our motives. He is like a wise parent who isn't going to give us what we want, when we want it. Although He is aware of our desires, He is not going to throw them at us to make us happy. He gives us what is necessary in His time. He is always testing us, trying to produce character and His vision in our hearts. I don't know about you, but I'm glad I did not always get what I wanted. And I'm glad that when I did get what I wanted, it came in His timing and therefore with His blessing.

> "So Hannah arose after they had finished eating and drinking in Shiloh. Now Eli the priest was sitting on the seat by the doorpost of the tabernacle of the Lord. And she was in bitterness of soul, and prayed to the Lord and wept in anguish."[19]

Let's look at "bitterness of soul." Bitterness in our souls can be a dangerous. We can be so focused on our desires and longings that we become bitter. We can become bitter when we have not forgiven someone who hurt us. Maybe that someone is your rival. The soul is the place in which our emotions, imagination, intellect, will, and even selfish thoughts can take over if we are not careful. God created us with a spirit, soul and body. The spirit is redeemed once we receive Jesus as our savior. The soul is always warring against the spirit to lead.

Can you imagine Hannah at the altar crying bitterly before the Lord because she longed for a child? Year after year, her rival became pregnant and gave birth. With each child came a great reminder that she was not a mother. I know many women who are "Hannahs"—waiting, anticipating, counting days, taking one pregnancy test after another. Many give up and choose another way to have children. Others long and become bitter in their soul.

We wait, anticipate, and count days in many areas of our lives. There always seems to be that place deep inside that feels taunted—that place of great longing. We may not like our present situation, and we may feel that God isn't being fair, so we become bitter. We cross our arms and demand a change. Yet, once the longing produces bitterness, bitterness produces anger, resentment, and jealousy.

As I write this, I am laughing to myself because I have been there. Many times, I prayed in church or even at home. I grieved and cried about circumstances and issues that were beyond my control to change. I knew God could change them, but it didn't seem like God and I were on the same page, let alone the same timeline.

There were times when I was so bitter, I just cried. These are the times when you need God to answer; when you need a breakthrough;

when you want it bad enough you don't care what you look like to other people. No one knows your pain or even the details of your circumstance. People can watch and talk, and they do.

But then, something happens in the hearts. That bitterness leaves, and then we have hope. The scripture says, "So Hannah ate. Then she pulled herself together, slipped away quietly, and entered the sanctuary."[20] She made a vow and said, "O LORD of hosts, if You will indeed look on the affliction of Your maidservant and remember me, and not forget Your maidservant, but will give Your maidservant a male child, then I will give him to the LORD all the days of his life, and no razor shall come upon his head."[21]

What happened? This sounds like a different person. Hannah's tears of bitterness turned to words of faith, joy, patience, wisdom and trust. She now had what she needed to see her process to the end. Hannah had a new perspective on her afflictions. The desire and longing for a child was still there, but somehow, she received a revelation about what God was up to. You see, we can be too focused on ourselves. We want our stuff, and we want it our way. God does care about our desires, and it is His pleasure that we have life and have it more abundantly. In addition to our earthly desires, His Kingdom is forever advancing, and sometimes these desires are tied to something bigger than our NOW. They need to be presented in the right time and season.

The story continues:

> "And it happened, as she continued praying before the LORD, that Eli watched her mouth. Now Hannah spoke in her heart; only her lips moved, but her voice was not heard. Therefore, Eli thought she was drunk. So Eli said

to her, "How long will you be drunk? Put your wine away from you!"²²

How many times have you been hurt about something and you were not acting like yourself? How many times were you pondering something in your heart and couldn't say a word? It happens to us all the time and we can't explain it to others. My husband would say to me, "Audra, are you okay?" "Yes," I would reply. Then he would say, "Are we okay?" "Yes," I would answer. Then he would say, "Are the kids okay?" and I would reply, "Yes." "Then what is bothering you?"

It is easy to misinterpret the actions of others. Their lack of response or weeping are not always bad. Furthermore, their actions might not have anything to do with you or the people around. Just as the priest Eli assumed that Hannah was drunk, others can assume the worst about us. Hannah was so wrapped up in her situation that she had no idea that she looked drunk. Here was her response:

> "But Hannah answered and said, 'No, my lord, I am a woman of sorrowful spirit. I have drunk neither wine nor intoxicating drink, but have poured out my soul before the LORD. Do not consider your maidservant a wicked woman, for out of the abundance of my complaint and grief I have spoken until now.'"

Oh boy! We don't always know the story behind someone's tears. We don't always know why people are coming to church and what they are looking for. We don't know why our neighbors do not come out of their homes. We get so worried when we see people who don't look as clean as they should. They don't worship like we do. We make judgements about people based on some rumors we have heard. We think we know, but sometimes we don't. I have been wrong about people, and others have been wrong about me. But God's grace is sufficient for all people and situations. Hannah said, "I'm not drunk but grieved, and I am pouring out my soul to God." We have to come to terms with our longing and say, "I don't care what people think." We need God to do something now.

As a bystander, we can refuse to get involved, or we can pray with them. Praying is more powerful and effective. Eli, after hearing her story, put himself in agreement with what she was praying for and said, "'Go in peace, and the God of Israel grant your petition which you have asked of Him.' And she said, 'Let your maidservant find favor in your sight.' So the woman went her way and ate, and her face was no longer sad." Once she got it all out of her system, she was no longer sad. She got up and ate, and her face (perspective) changed.

SAMUEL IS BORN AND DEDICATED

> "Then they rose early in the morning and worshiped before the LORD, and returned and came to their house at Ramah. And Elkanah knew Hannah his wife, and the LORD remembered her."[25]

God has not forgotten your prayers. He does not overlook your tears. He did not walk away when you were hurt. He is fully aware of the abuse and tainted relationships. He was there when you did not get the job. He was there when you miscarried, and He is there now. The Message version of 1 Samuel 1:19 says, "Up before dawn, they worshiped God and returned home to Ramah. Elkanah slept with Hannah his wife, and God began making the necessary arrangements in response to what she had asked." God heard her cry and responded when it was time. Could it be that today God is "making the necessary arrangements in response" to what you have asked?

> "So it came to pass in the process of time that Hannah conceived and bore a son, and called his name Samuel, saying, 'Because I have asked for him from the Lord.'"[26]

Can you say, "process of time?" The process takes time. God always has a process for answering our prayers. He knows our hearts, motives and when we are ready.

Now let's finish the story:

> "Now the man Elkanah and all his house went up to offer to the Lord the yearly sacrifice and his vow. But Hannah did not go up, for she said to her husband, 'Not until the child is weaned; then I will take him, that he may appear before the Lord and remain there forever.'
>
> So Elkanah her husband said to her, 'Do what seems best to you; wait until you have weaned him. Only let the Lord establish His word.' Then the woman stayed and nursed her son until she had weaned him.
>
> Now when she had weaned him, she took him up with her, with three bulls, one ephah of flour, and a skin of wine, and brought him to the house of the Lord in Shiloh. And the child was young. Then they slaughtered a bull, and brought the child to Eli. And she said, 'O my lord! As your soul lives, my lord, I am the woman who stood by you here, praying to the Lord. For this child I prayed, and the Lord has granted me my petition which I asked of Him. Therefore, I also have lent him to the Lord; as long as he lives he shall be lent to the Lord.' So they worshiped the Lord there."[27]

There is a time when we have to "wean" our own plans, just as we have to wean our children. Weaning isn't easy. I nursed all five of my children, and when it was time to wean them, it was always hard for both me and the baby. However, I knew it was time. Hannah not only weaned Samuel, she saw that his life would be more profitable for God's kingdom than her need to raise him. Because God gave her what she asked for, she honored her word and brought Samuel to the temple and into the hands of Eli and his corrupt sons. I can't imagine how difficult that must have been.

God was aware Hannah was barren. He was aware she greatly desired a child. He was aware of the tormenting rival. He was aware of the great lament she had over her situation, but God was also aware of His timing. All the while, God was taking Hannah through the process of obtaining the promise He was also taking Israel through a process.

This wasn't a good time for Israel. A "word from the Lord was rare in those days, visions were infrequent."[28] Men were not listening to God at that time, and God did not speak very often. This "silence" is often a form of divine judgment, and if not broken, would prove to be Israel's undoing (see 1 Samuel 28; Psalm 74:9; Isaiah 29:9-14; Micah 3:6-7; also Proverbs 29:18). We are told that prophecy was rare, so that we see the calling of Samuel as an end to God's silence (see 1 Samuel 3:19-21)."[29] Samuel needed to be born and raised during that specific time. He would be the prophet in the land through whom God spoke.

The process God is taking you through is never just for you. You may feel as if you are isolated and alone. You might not know all the details, but God does, and He knows how our response to the process will ultimately affect us and someone else. He promised us that He would work everything out for our good and His glory. Again, the process takes time.

ACTIVATION #1

1. Draw a timeline. Start with your estimated conception date (approximately 9 months before your birth date). Put points, dots, or stars, to signify important dates, i.e., birthday, first day of school, baptism day, the day you were saved, graduation, marriage, birth of children, etc.
2. Write a short description about that day. Do you remember what you were wearing, where you were, who was around, and why that day was special?
3. If you can, pinpoint what you felt God was saying about that day.

ACTIVATION #2

1. List your rivals (unhealthy and unnecessary rivals). Write their names and what the competition was about. Forgive!
2. Ask God to show you when He was making you wait and you complained. Do you see it was better to wait? Did God remove the situation or person because it wasn't good for you? Thank God that He has the perfect timing.

ACTIVATION PRAYER

Dear Lord, thank you for always having my best interest in mind. Thank you for the day I was conceived and for protecting me in my mother's womb. Thank you for pinpointing various events in my life where You were present and teaching me. I choose to forgive my rivals, and I ask You to forgive me for the times I was a rival to others. Thank you for making me wait for the things I was not ready for, and thank you for removing the things that were not good for me. Help me to remember Your process takes time, and that you are aware of all the details. Prepare me for what is next in my life. In Jesus' name, Amen!

CHAPTER 3
God's view

"Then God said, 'Let Us make man in Our image, according to Our likeness; let them have dominion over the fish of the sea, over the birds of the air, and over the cattle, over all the earth and over every creeping thing that creeps on the earth.' So God created man in His own image; in the image of God He created him; male and female He created them."[1]

GOD'S MIRROR IMAGE

God created mankind, male and female in His own image. We are unlike the animals, plants, or trees on the earth. God spoke everything into existence with exception of man. Man is God's very special creation in which He breathed the breath of life into. God is spirit without a human form. Jesus was given a human form to enter the earth for the redemption of mankind.

the process

Before God created anything, He loved and chose us in Christ. "Even before he made the world, God loved us and chose us in Christ to be holy and without fault in His eyes."[2] Can you imagine? God had you and me in mind before He made the world. And when He created us, He created us in His very own image and likeness. Let's explore a couple of words.

Image:
1. a physical likeness or representation of a person, animal, or thing, photographed, painted, sculptured, or otherwise made visible.
2. an optical counterpart or appearance of an object, as is produced by reflection from a mirror, refraction by a lens, or the passage of luminous rays through a small aperture and their reception on a surface.
3. a mental representation; idea; conception.[3]

An image has a visible physical likeness. It is an optical counterpart made by a reflection. It is an idea or concept.

Likeness:
1. the condition of being alike; similarity
2. a painted, carved, molded, or graphic image of a person or thing
3. an imitative appearance.[4]

God made a visible physical or graphic image, likeness, and similarity of Himself reflecting Himself and His appearance and it is you. This was already an idea or concept before He ever created the earth. God's image can also be seen in His attributes and His creations. An attribute is something that belongs to a person, thing, group, etc.; a quality, character, characteristic, or property.[5]

GOD'S IMAGE, OUR IDENTITY

It is important to know some of God's attributes because they help us have a better understanding of ourselves. We should strive to align our behavior with the attributes of God's image. Though these are not all the attributes to be considered the following are the most relevant to this discussion: Spoken word-language, creativity, love, holiness-the standard, and mercy.

1. Spoken Word-Language

"Language: A system for the expression of thoughts, feelings, etc., by the use of spoken sounds or conventional symbols."[6]

> "In the beginning God created the heavens and the earth. The earth was without form, and void; and darkness was on the face of the deep. And the Spirit of God was hovering over the face of the waters. Then God said, 'Let there be light'; and there was light. And God saw the light, that it was good; and God divided the light from the darkness. God called the light Day, and the darkness He called Night. So the evening and the morning were the first day."[7]

God began His creation by using spoken sounds, words. "Then God said, 'Let there be…'" What was spoken came into being. God used His spoken language to show us how important our spoken words are. Our spoken words actually create. We can speak blessing or curses, life or death, but these words create something in the atmosphere.

God said His creation was "good" and He named everything He created. "God called the light Day and the darkness he called Night..." God continued to speak and create. He created the entire universe just by speaking.

Verse 26, is key in our discussion of identity. God said, "Let Us make man in Our image, according to Our likeness."[8] "Our" refers to God the father, God the Son who is Jesus, and God the Holy Spirit. Let's read what John Rendle Short wrote in an article for *Answers in Genesis* called, "Man: The Image of God."

> "Another reason we know about the three (the Trinity), is because there is communication between the persons. 'The Lord said...' we read in Genesis 1:3; to whom did he speak? It could only have been to another member of the Trinity. As soon as man was created God spoke to him. Constantly throughout Scripture we read the phrase, 'The word of the Lord...' For this reason, the Bible is known as the word of God. As though to underline the importance of communication, God sent his son Jesus Christ into the world with the name Logos or the 'Word.' John writes, 'In the beginning was the Word and the Word was with God, and the Word was God. All things were made by him, and without him was not anything made that was made...'[9] So there is the written word (the Bible), and the living Word (Jesus Christ)."[10]

2. Creativity

Creativity is "the process by which one utilizes creative ability."[11] My daughters are great artists. They are able to paint and draw using a variety of media. From ink to charcoal, watercolor to oil, they create some of the most beautiful pictures, full of detail. I love to see the color palettes they choose for each picture. Sometimes there is a running theme for a series of pictures, and sometimes the picture stands out on its own conveying a specific message.

It is easy to see that God shows His creativity in nature. If you have ever been to a museum or looked at an outdoor magazine, there is evidence of God's creativity in many paintings and photographs. Did you know that God gave you a creative capacity? Look at your gifts and hobbies. Do you write music or lyrics? Are you an artist or architect? Can you design clothes? While we can be inspired by God's beautiful landscapes and be inspired to be creative, God was inspired by Himself, and therefore used His spoken word to be creative.

3. Love

Love: "to have a profoundly tender, passionate affection for."[12] It isn't hard to understand love. We often think about what and who we love, as well as who loves us. We think about our parent's love, the love between couples, the love of siblings, and the love of our pets. But the love of God is steadfast, eternal, and never changing, simply because He is love. "Beloved, let us love one another, for love is from God, and whoever loves has been born of God and knows God. Anyone who does not love does not know God, because God is love."[13] The best way to see God's love for us is in this next verse: "God shows His love for us in that while we were still sinners, Christ died for us."[14]

Dying for someone is a sacrificial love. Many of us will never have to make such a sacrifice. We will live, get old, and die. We all know at least one person who serves in the military. They are willing to put themselves at death's door because they love this country and the freedoms it affords us all. They don't need to have a personal relationship with us, but the love for the country equips and gives them courage to serve, even to the point of death. Paul writes a powerful statement in Ephesians about a sacrificial love of a husband for his wife in relation to Christ and the church:

> "Husbands, love your wives [seek the highest good for her and surround her with a caring, unselfish love], just as Christ also loved the church and gave Himself up for her, so that He might sanctify the church, having cleansed her by the washing of water with the word [of God], so that [in turn] He might present the church to Himself in glorious splendor, without spot or wrinkle or any such thing; but that she would be holy [set apart for God] and blameless. Even so husbands should and are morally obligated to love their own wives as [being in a sense] their own bodies. He who loves his own wife loves himself. For no one ever hated his own body, but [instead] he nourishes and protects and cherishes it, just as Christ does the church."[15]

Christ "gave Himself up for the her, the church." This is sacrificial love at its best. This kind of love is the reason we are here today. Christ willfully took the penalty of death for us. Love never fails.

4. Holiness – The Standard

Holiness: "the quality or state of being holy; sanctity."[16] It is hard to believe that God calls us, flawed people, to be holy. God is holy, unlike any other and without sin. This is what separates His holiness from that which He has called us to. Often the word holy drives the believer to a place of perfection that we cannot attain in and of ourselves.

> "When Peter repeats the Lord's words in 1 Peter 1:16, he is talking specifically to believers. As believers, we need to

be 'set apart' from the world unto the Lord. We need to be living by God's standards, not the world's. God isn't calling us to be perfect, but to be distinct from the world. 1 Peter 2:9 describes believers as 'a holy nation.' It is a fact! We are separated from the world; we need to live out that reality in our day-to-day lives, which Peter tells us how to do in 1 Peter 1:13-16."[17]

In the next chapter we will talk about the mask of perfection. Perfection does not leave room for God to tweak us. In the above scripture, Peter is stating we are to be "set apart," not striving for perfection. Separating ourselves from the mindsets of the world helps us the live our lives in reality, not perfectionism. This should be our standard. This is called holiness.

5. Mercy

Mercy: "compassionate or kindly forbearance shown toward an offender, an enemy, or other person in one's power; compassion, pity, or benevolence."[18]

> "The LORD, the LORD, a God merciful and gracious, slow to anger, and abounding in steadfast love and faithfulness, keeping steadfast love for thousands, forgiving iniquity and transgression and sin, but who will by no means clear the guilty, visiting the iniquity of the fathers on the children and the children's children, to the third and the fourth generation."[19]

I love this scripture. God described more of His attributes to us. Look at the words He chose. Merciful, gracious, slow to anger, steadfast love, faithful, forgiving, righteous judge. The first word is "merciful." If God is merciful and He knows all sin and even sent His only son to die for the sins of the world, then how much mercy should we show to others. We can show mercy for others even if we don't agree with their lifestyles or actions. Mercy should be extended over judgment.

> "Paul's discussions of the new man and old man give us great insight into what it means to be created in the image and likeness of God.[20] It is an image that bears the righteousness and holiness of God. When Scripture describes all of God's attributes, it is in the context of God being the perfection of such attributes. For example, God is love, and God's love is perfect. Humanity shares many of God's attributes, and we were originally created to reflect God's perfect character in righteousness and holiness. While God has character traits that He does not share with humanity (e.g., God is self-existent, omniscient, omnipotent), we can still see His shared attributes in humanity today, even though they are distorted by sin. Attributes such as love, self-awareness, justice, grace, and mercy are distinct from attributes associated with animals. They are part of the very being of humanity."[21]

> "But we all, with unveiled face, beholding as in a mirror the glory of the Lord are being transformed into the same image from glory to glory, just as from the Lord, the Spirit."[22]

IDENTITY IS BUILT ON TRUE FOUNDATION

Now that we have established certain truths about our identity we can begin to see how much God cares about each of us. God chose humanity, not the flowers, animals, the oceans or even the beautiful mountains, to show His reflection on earth. Identity is built on God's image and God's attributes. This revelation knowledge gives us a true foundation for our identity. These truths will anchor our new perspective on who we are. Identity should be connected to truth. Identity is "the state of having unique identifying characteristics held by no other person or thing; the individual characteristics by which a person or thing is recognized; individuality, personality, distinctiveness, uniqueness."[23] What does this definition of identity say about our identity in Christ? We should be recognized by our unique identifying character and attributes because they come from our unique and distinct God.

God created only one of you, and there will never be another. Your DNA and fingerprint are unique to you. You were perfectly made in the womb of your mother by God. When a parent looks at their children, they want to see some reflection of their character and all they have invested. Similarly, you have a distinct personality which should reflect the character of God; so that upon examination, God should observe some remnants of Himself.

Once you have received Christ into your heart and have accepted His sacrifice and the shedding of His blood for your sins, you are a new creature, a new creation. You display God's glory and reflect His goodness. "I have been crucified with Christ; and it is no longer I who live, but Christ lives in me; and the life which I now live in the flesh I live by faith in the Son of God who loved me and gave himself up for me."[24] "Therefore if anyone is in Christ, he is a new creature; the old things passed away; behold, new things have come."[25] God has given you a new identity because you are a new creation in Christ. This identity establishes you in His truth.

The culture gives labels that divide people into identity groups. Living in an American society as an African-American Christian woman, I have been given many labels by the culture. Some labels I identify with, while others I do not. I have also received labels from different social groups with whom I associate. We give labels to others based on their career, their political affiliations, their church denominations, and for so many other reasons. What are the labels that have been given to you? Do you identify with them?

My identity foundation in Christ is far more important. It is where I will discover my purpose, passions, and place in the body of Christ as well as the society. My heritage, history, ethnicity, gender, and my educational and religious associations are unique to me. They are jewels in my crown and add to my individuality. Knowing the truth of your identity in Christ makes it possible to move beyond the glass ceiling of our culture.

CULTURAL STANDARDS AND BEAUTY

Throughout history, every culture has had its own standard for identity. That standard is used to group people based on status, beauty, privilege and brings separation. Men and women alike have had to conform to these standards and have done so at a great cost. In this next portion of this chapter we are going to look at a couple of cultures that have misused others to uphold certain standards which help them to gain privilege and status.

It is common for a culture to identify people by their social, economic, religious, political, and even educational affiliations. The problem is that most often people feel as if they are being divided and even devalued. Certain beauty traits were used to separate royalty and common people. The color of skin, shape and size of a nose, texture of hair, just to name a few traits, were used to divide people into superior and inferior groups. These distinct traits were used to justify slavery and genocide. Certain traits and beauty standards were sought after and cherished by many, even at the cost of sacrificed freedom or mutilation. Ways of getting status and privilege were often inhuman. We can see some examples in biblical history:

> "Now it came to pass in the days of Ahasuerus (this was the Ahasuerus who reigned over one hundred and twenty-seven provinces, from India to Ethiopia), in those days when King Ahasuerus sat on the throne of his kingdom, which was in Shushan the citadel, that in the third year of his reign he made a feast for all his officials and servants—the powers of Persia and Media, the nobles, and the princes of the provinces being before him—when he showed the riches of his glorious kingdom and the splendor of his excellent majesty for many days, one hundred and eighty days in all.
>
> And when these days were completed, the king made a feast lasting seven days for all the people who were present in Shushan the citadel, from great to small, in the court of the garden of the king's palace. There were white and blue linen curtains fastened with cords of fine linen and purple on silver rods and marble pillars; and the couches were of gold and silver on a mosaic pavement of alabaster, turquoise, and white and black marble. And they served drinks in golden vessels, each vessel being different from the other, with royal wine in abundance, according to the generosity of the king. In accordance with the law, the drinking was not compulsory; for so the king had ordered all the officers of his household, that they should do according to each man's pleasure. Queen Vashti also made a feast for the women in the royal palace which belonged to King Ahasuerus.

the process

> On the seventh day, when the heart of the king was merry with wine, he commanded Mehuman Biztha, Harbona, Bigtha, Abagtha, Zethar, and Carcas, seven eunuchs who served in the presence of King Ahasuerus, to bring Queen Vashti before the king, wearing her royal crown, in order to show her beauty to the people and the officials, for she was beautiful to behold. But Queen Vashti refused to come at the king's command brought by his eunuchs; therefore, the king was furious, and his anger burned within him."[26]

King Ahasuerus wants to display his whole kingdom to the nobles and princes. Gold, silver, precious stones, linens, and artifacts surround the palace. The King's possessions included his queen, Vashti. She is a part of his kingdom, and she is his property. Her position as queen depended on how she pleased the king, her husband.

Queen Vashti, who was also hosting a feast for the women, refuses for her own reasons to not present herself to the king and his guest. This act of defiance fuels the anger of the King. Although the reason for Vashti's refusal is unknown, I can only imagine, given the circumstances, that she did not want to be viewed as an object or humiliated in any way, because after all, she was the queen. The fact that her beauty is mentioned and the King is displaying his grand kingdom suggests that Queen Vashti knows the intentions are not to honor her as queen, but to display her as the King's property. Queen Vashti is also familiar with how the women are treated in the palace, for she herself is a part of a harem, although she holds the title of queen.

There is nothing wrong with being known for your beauty (beautiful teeth, beautiful eyes, beautiful smile, the most beautiful woman in the world, etc.). Queen Vashti is called beautiful. Many women in our culture have been noted for their beauty: Sophia Loren, Naomi Campbell, and Iman, to name a few. God created beautiful things and people. The issue isn't beauty, but identity.

Many have been identified and admired because of a particular physical attribute. Look at models, celebrates or even body builders. They are seen as the standard in our culture. Others strive and spend lots of money to mimic their ideal look because they think it will make them more important in the society. Skin color, eye color, length of hair, size of lips, and others physical characteristics have become a standard to uphold. Yet there are others who have been shunned because of their odd physical appearance. The Freak Shows are great examples of people being exploited. However, our true identity does not come from our outward appearance, but the fact that we were created in the image of God. "Charm is deceitful and beauty is passing, but a woman who fears the Lord, she shall be praised."[2]

> "Then the king's attendants, who served him, said, 'Let beautiful young virgins be sought for the king. Let the king appoint administrators in all the provinces of his kingdom, and have them gather all the beautiful young virgins to the citadel in Susa, into the harem, under the custody of Hegai, the king's eunuch, who is in charge of the women; and let their beauty preparations be given to them. Then let the young woman who pleases the king be queen in place of Vashti.' This pleased the king, and he did accordingly."[28]

A harem is the part of the palace where the King's wives live; the wives of a man who has several wives. Ancient kings often had many wives. Solomon had 700, and also 300 other women who lived with him. The men who looked after a harem were called eunuchs.[29]

the process

Many cultures made men eunuchs even as little boys. Often when there was a war and prisoners were taken, the young men were castrated and used as eunuchs. Young men were taken from their families as was their right to produce children of their own. We can see in this story that there were eunuchs who served the king as well as the harem.

The young virgins were sought after throughout the kingdom and brought into a harem. These young virgins did not have a choice, and their lives would forever change. There could only be one queen, but those who pleased the King were retained to serve him sexually and in any way they were useful to the kingdom at large. Most of these girls would never return home, and many would never see their families again.

> "Now when it was each young woman's turn to go before King Ahasuerus, after the end of her twelve months under the regulations for the women—for the days of their beautification were completed as follows: six months with oil of myrrh and six months with [sweet] spices and perfumes and the beauty preparations for women—then the young woman would go before the king in this way: anything that she wanted was given her to take with her from the harem into the king's palace. In the evening, she would go in and the next morning she would return to the second harem, to the custody of Shaashgaz, the king's eunuch who was in charge of the concubines. She would not return to the king unless he delighted in her and she was summoned by name."[30]

As a former spa owner, I wanted every client to receive a relaxing treatment that would have a lasting impression on them. The rooms were filled with the sweet smells of oils and herbs, the treatment beds were covered with the finest linen, and the sound of soft spa music would calm even the most agitated soul. But this was not a spa experience for these young women. This was more of a quarantine, to make sure they were properly screened for any type of defect or disease.

> "But according to some, the initial six-month treatment with oil of myrrh was meant to purify her. They say that oil of myrrh was commonly used for antiseptic and antifungal purposes and as a deodorant. Therefore, the first six months of her preparation were for cleansing, healing and purification. Once they were certain she was free of disease they spent the next 6 months maximizing her beauty. So the idea being conveyed in Esther is that purification precedes beautification." [31]

There are many examples throughout history that regarded women as property. They were misused and mistreated for the status and wealth of others. Within various communities, rich and poor alike, there was always a standard of beauty. I remember doing a research paper in high school about different cultures. In my research, I came across pictures of shoes worn by Chinese women. They were so tiny. At first, I thought they were the shoes of little girls or even dolls. I later found out they were the shoes of grown women. My next thought was that they were really small and petite people. Researching further and seeing more pictures of a human feet, whose toes were wrapped under the arc brought tears to my eyes.

In some Chinese cultures, women had their feet bound as a symbol of wealth and status. It was a painful sight to see, and even more painful to hear the documented accounts of women who were still alive today, even though the practice has been long gone.

the process

The process of binding feet (also known as "lotus feet") started before the arch had a chance to fully develop, when the girls were somewhere between the ages of four and nine. After soaking in warm water, herbs, and animal blood, the toes would be curled over to the sole of the foot and bound with tightly with cotton bandages. The toes and arch would be broken with force—unbound, rebound, then rebound more tightly and repeated as many times as necessary. The girl's mother, grandmother, and other sisters alike would perform the gruesome task. The tradition is thought to have originated among the upper-class court dancers in Imperial China around the 10th century, before spreading to the lower classes. Naturally affecting their ability to walk, it came to be seen as a sign of wealth—after all, the wealthiest of people didn't need to walk or work in fields.

> "Yang's mother began tightly binding her feet with strips of cloth when she was just six years old, forcibly folding the youngster's four smallest toes under the soles and deliberately, over time, breaking delicate bones to mold each foot into the shape of a so-called 'golden lotus,' revered for centuries as the epitome of feminine beauty, refinement, even sexual attractiveness. Further squeezed and sculpted by hand to create a high arch and a hoof-like appearance, Yang's shattered feet would set that way, and remain deformed for life. 'It was so painful, but my mother said that if I didn't do it I would never find a husband, nobody would have me,' says the widowed mother of four. 'It wasn't a strange thing to do in those days—many girls in Liuyi had small feet. The tradition was strong here. If your feet were small, you were admired, you were special.' says Yang Zhaoshi."[32]

I was amazed at how their feet looked like the hooves of an animal. How did this become such a statement for beauty? Who could have decided this was a respectable tradition for young girls to maintain status and beauty? It is very sad, indeed, to wonder how many women suffered before they perfected their method.

TODAY'S CULTURAL IDENTITY

I said earlier that I owned a spa. It was a wellness spa, whose primary focus was aiding the body in the healing and detoxification process. Holistic nutritionists and wellness practitioners would evaluate and screen clients, then recommend a wellness therapy which included nutritional supplements, dietary instructions, herbal detoxification, as well as body contour wraps.

As a licensed esthetician and professional makeup artist, I was trained to look at the skin in efforts to transform it. It was important that I analyze the skin correctly so I could recommend treatment and products that would make the skin flawless. We sold a lot of skincare and makeup. Everyone was trying to make their skin appear flawless by covering any imperfections, making it look younger and radiant so they could feel good about their appearance.

Beauty is a multi-billion-dollar industry with products, treatments, surgeries, therapies, and millions of physical locations throughout the international communities, all searching for the fountain of youth—a never ending beauty fairytale. Our wellness spa was on the cutting edge, and we were able to help many clients reach their optimum health through our services. It was a joy every time a client came in for their weekly consultation to see them reach their goals. Our number one service was the detoxification/contour body wrap. It produced great results in hours, with each client losing two to four inches, throughout their entire body, with each wrap. This loss was not water loss but waste being eliminated through the lymphatic system and bowels. You can imagine the number of wraps we did a day for satisfied customers.

Sadly, the initial consultation before the series of wraps, revealed many things. One, was that most clients hated their body type. In the years we offered the service, I never had one client tell me they loved their body and only wanted the health benefits of the wrap. All my clients, men included, wanted to improve the appearance of their body in some area and were their body's own worst critic. I had a huge clientele of dancers and athletes alike who really didn't have many visible signs of aging or loss of elasticity. They were very fit and toned, with minimum cellulite. But they were often the most disgruntled about their appearance. I said this to say, a person's physical appearance does not determine their satisfaction and contentment. We may look at a person and think he or she has an amazing body, skin, hair, etc., but each person struggles with their own self-perception.

As their practitioner, it was my job to get clients to see the positive changes that each service brought. Our average weight loss with this program for men was thirty pounds and for women fifteen pounds, in a 30-day period. At the end of the day, this was the reason most people came to us. The health benefits of sleeping better, having more energy, loss of craving, mental clarity and much more were just added bonuses for most.

The painful truth of being in the beauty industry was that cultural beauty often defined the identity of that person, even among Christians. It seems that whether we are tall, short, skinny, overweight, blond, bald, of European or African descent, rich, poor, educated, churched or not, the focus on physical appearance takes precedence over our identity in Christ. I would say that we as a culture would rather spend billions of dollars on personal beauty enhancements than investing in the many tools that build our character. Our search for the "fountain of youth" overrides the need to teach our sons and daughters the significance of finding pleasure and security in a God who loves them and made them for His glory. I wonder, dear friend, if we have lost balance.

Balance is good. I am not at all against makeup, exercise, or certain beauty enhancements. I choose myself to wear makeup and keep my weight under control. I, like many, enjoy compliments. But my identity is wrapped up in one question: Can God, the one who created me, see His reflection in me? The fear of the Lord goes a long way and brings wisdom and balance. When I reverence God with awe and wonder my focus isn't solely on what is temporary but what is eternal.

I assure you, God knows everything about you—all you are and all you will be. Nothing can hide you from His presence. God's view of you is His delight. He has invested so much in you and what He has in store for you, but you will only know and experience it by allowing Him to have access to you. It is your choice: "Look at me. I stand at the door. I knock. If you hear me call and open the door, I'll come right in and sit down to supper with you."[33]

Dear friend, God is already in your neighborhood. He is already walking up the path to your house. Now He is standing at your door, ready to knock. Will you let Him in, or will you close the curtains and stand there holding your breath until He leaves? Are you working on your character, or is getting to the desired weight more important? Loose or gain the weight you need to maintain a

the process

healthy lifestyle but work on developing your character. God made you a beautiful creation. In the next three chapters, we are going to look at what causes us to forget that God's image is our identity. I want to close this chapter with one of my favorite scriptures in the Bible, Psalm 139:

> "O Lord, you have searched me [thoroughly] and have known me. You know when I sit down and when I rise up [my entire life, everything I do]; You understand my thought from afar. You scrutinize my path and my lying down, and You are intimately acquainted with all my ways. Even before there is a word on my tongue [still unspoken], Behold, O Lord, You know it all.
>
> You have enclosed me behind and before, and [You have] placed Your hand upon me. Such [infinite] knowledge is too wonderful for me; It is too high [above me], I cannot reach it. Where can I go from Your Spirit? Or where can I flee from Your presence? If I ascend to heaven, You are there; If I make my bed in Sheol (the nether world, the place of the dead), behold, You are there. If I take the wings of the dawn, If I dwell in the remotest part of the sea, even there Your hand will lead me, and Your right hand will take hold of me. If I say, 'Surely the darkness will cover me, And the night will be the only light around me,' even the darkness is not dark to You and conceals nothing from You, but the night shines as bright as the day; darkness and light are alike to You.
>
> For You formed my innermost parts; You knit me [together] in my mother's womb. I will give thanks and praise to You, for I am fearfully and wonderfully made;

wonderful are Your works, and my soul knows it very well. My frame was not hidden from You, When I was being formed in secret, and intricately and skillfully formed [as if embroidered with many colors] in the depths of the earth. Your eyes have seen my unformed substance; and in Your book were all written. The days that were appointed for me, when as yet there was not one of them [even taking shape].

How precious also are Your thoughts to me, O God! How vast is the sum of them! If I could count them, they would outnumber the sand. When I awake, I am still with You. O that You would kill the wicked, O God; Go away from me, therefore, men of bloodshed. For they speak against You wickedly, Your enemies take Your name in vain. Do I not hate those who hate You, O Lord? And do I not loathe those who rise up against You? I hate them with perfect and utmost hatred; they have become my enemies.

Search me [thoroughly], O God, and know my heart; test me and know my anxious thoughts; and see if there is any wicked or hurtful way in me, and lead me in the everlasting way."[34]

ACTIVATION

Write Psalm 139 in a journal, and be creative. Read it every day until you find pure peace and joy in who you are, in Jesus. Here are a few more scriptures to think about:

> "Before I was born the Lord called me; from my birth, he has made mention of my name."[35]

> "Before I formed you in the womb I knew you before you were born I sanctified you."[36]

ACTIVATION PRAYER

Father God, I thank you for loving me so much that You created me in Your very own image and likeness. I thank you that I was on Your heart before You created the earth. I thank you that my identity in You has nothing to do with my personal appearance or the things in my past, but I am a new creation in Christ Jesus.

Please forgive me for the times my focus was on myself and out of balance. I have heard You knock at my door many times before. Forgive me for not letting You in, out of fear that You wouldn't like what You saw. I choose now to open the door. I am inviting You in to sit with me and tell me what You have in store for me. I want to be transparent with You, hiding nothing in my heart or mind. I want You to search me and point out those things in me that don't reflect Your image.

God's view

I thank you that I am fearfully and wonderfully made, every part of me. My physical, emotional, and spiritual person is marvelously made. Come in Lord Jesus, come in.

CHAPTER 4
unmask

It is believed that masquerades originated in West Africa. The French word is pronounced "mascarde" and "maschera" in Italian. The purpose for masquerades was a form of "masked" comedy, which was popular in many cultures throughout Europe, England, the Caribbean and southeastern United States during the 18th century. Masquerades were performed by masked characters during carnival celebrations and festivals. Carnivals were fun for the public but the wealthy would attend masquerade balls. These balls were extravagant with music, dancing and parades to display the fun of the occasion. Marti Gras in Louisiana, is an example of a masquerade parade.

Typical costumes for these masquerades varied from culture to culture but all included masks of some sort. A mask usually depicted a historical character. The performer would tell the story of long forgotten heroes. Mask makers had a special place in the society.

the process

They created masks from their imagination and usually used a variety of fabric, feathers and paints. Masks had many uses including expressing creativity, hiding identity, and voicing emotions and opinions without judgment. In the famous play, Romeo and Juliet by Shakespeare, Romeo meets Juliet at a masquerade ball.

While masquerades can be full of fun and creativity, we are going to be talking about unmasking. Unmasking ourselves so that others can see our gifts, true identity and purpose, can be very frightening. Masks cover us and our issues we are not willing to face. We may spend years masquerading around, trying to pretend we are fine. Remember one of the reasons people used masks during a masquerade was to hide identity. We are going to discuss the reasons we mask ourselves in the first place.

Let's start by asking ourselves the question: what is a mask?

1. "A mask is a piece of cloth or other material, which you wear over your face so that people cannot see who you are, or so that you look like someone or something else.
2. A mask is a piece of cloth or other material that you wear over all or part of your face to protect you from germs or harmful substances.
3. If you describe someone's behavior as a mask, you mean that they do not show their real feelings or character.
4. If you mask your feelings, you deliberately do not show them in your behavior, so that people cannot know what you really feel.
5. If one thing masks another, it prevents people from noticing or recognizing the other thing."[1]

I find that these descriptions of masks give us a basis for why we feel mask are necessary. There are practical reasons for wearing a mask. Some masks are for protecting the face or eyes so they don't get injured. We see this with fireman and those working with toxic chemicals. Even swimmers wear goggles to protect their eyes from the chlorinated water. There are also decorative masks that we use in drama, theater, and ballrooms extravaganzas. These can be kind of fun. Often, the villain in a story wears a mask like the Phantom in the *Phantom of the Opera*. Then of course, there are superhero masks, designed to conceal identity.

Concealing identity is usually why we wear emotional masks. We use emotional masks to hide our insecurities, to cover shame, to protect us when we are afraid, to appear perfect, or perhaps mask our hidden jealousies.

INSECURITIES

I was a late bloomer. I looked like a little girl until I was thirteen, and even then, I was still very petite. This was extremely difficult for me during middle school, because most of the girls were already developed. Gym class and the locker room were the worst places for me. I hated dressing in front of the girls for fear I would be teased about still wearing a training bra. I hid my insecurity by wearing one of my sister's bras to appear bigger and wearing warmup pants under my jeans. I thought the extra padding and volume would cover my awkwardness. Honestly, no one ever said a word to me about it. I was just "cute little Audra with the big brown eyes." I also hid my insecurities behind my gifts. I hid myself in my music, academics, and athleticism. This was the mask I was wearing.

The masks discussed in this chapter are the most common masks I see many women wear today. Most of the time, we are unaware that we have them on because they have become a normal part of our makeup and clothing habits. We will actually take them off at home, put them in our closet and grab them again the next morning. We put these masks on and off based on how we feel and the situation we find ourselves in. As we look at these masks together, I want us to examine our hearts.

Mask #1: Sparkly Silver Sins and Shame

Imagine a beautiful masquerade mask with sparkly diamonds, silver glitter, and eye holes just big enough to see where we are going, but distracting enough to cover what we are doing. Sometimes we mask ourselves because we are ashamed of our actions. Sin causes us to be ashamed. We can see this illustrated in the story of Adam and Eve.

> "Then the eyes of both of them were opened, and they realized they were naked; so they sewed fig leaves together and made coverings for themselves. Then the man and his wife heard the sound of the Lord God as he was walking in the garden in the cool of the day, and they hid from the Lord God among the trees of the garden. But the Lord God called to the man, 'Where are you?' He answered, 'I heard you in the garden, and I was afraid because I was naked; so I hid.' And he said, 'Who told you that you were naked? Have you eaten from the tree that I commanded you not to eat from?'"[2]

It's important to note that Adam knew they were naked. It was the tree they ate from that gave them knowledge of their nakedness, because God had never told them. Are you someone who has tasted the fruit from the forbidden tree? I'm sure we all have had a little taste here and there. There is something intriguing about having what we should not have.

Or, maybe you are someone who trusted the wisdom and advice of a friend, as Adam trusted Eve. I think we can all say "yes" to that as well. Adam and Eve made coverings for themselves to cover their nakedness, but the nakedness wasn't the problem. It was still just them and God in the garden. No one else was there to see them. They were really trying to cover their sin, which caused them to feel shame. They were in a place where they knew only God's holiness, goodness, grace, peace, love, and even His voice in the cool of the day. That was all they needed to know. Their innocence before God and each other was refreshing. But when they experienced sin, the atmosphere changed. It was quite different from what they had known before. Now there was fear, guilt, and shame. Their sin exposed their physical nakedness and spiritual vulnerability.

Innocent little children do not experience shame from their nakedness. They run around the house, the backyard, the kiddie pool and in and out of the bathtub, never thinking about the fact they are naked until their parent tells them to put on clothing. Once they are fitted with the proper clothing, they soon become aware that it is for protection. Adam and Eve's choice of clothing seemed to be sufficient at first, but as soon as they heard God, they felt exposed.

Their effort to cover their own sin may have been adequate for them, but it was insufficient in the presence of God. If their nakedness had solely been physical, the clothing would have been sufficient to cover their shame. The shame, however, was not merely physical, and neither was it just sin. It was also a spiritual act of defiance and disobedience against God.

First Adam and Eve covered themselves with fig leaves. Then God covered them with the skin of an innocent animal. Sure, the sacrifice of the innocent animal covered over the sin, but it did not cover the shame. Later, the lamb of God, Jesus, shed His blood to make an atonement for their sin. God's ideal clothing came at a price—the life of an innocent animal, who knew nothing about Adam and Eve and their sin. "Jesus who knew no sin became sin for us, that we might become the righteousness of God in Him."[3]

> "Now we know that if the earthly tent we live in is destroyed, we have a building from God, an eternal house in heaven, not built by human hands. Meanwhile we groan, longing to be clothed with our heavenly dwelling, because when we are clothed, we will not be found naked. For while we are in this tent, we groan and are burdened, because we do not wish to be unclothed but to be clothed with our heavenly dwelling, so that what is mortal may be swallowed up by life."[4]

God covered their shame by clothing them with His son's blood, which is necessary for our eternal stay in heaven. Many of us prefer to hide our sins with a mask instead of having them covered with the blood of Jesus. Let's look at how closely related nakedness and shame are in the Bible. Before Adam and Eve sinned, Genesis 2:25 says, "And they were both naked, the man and his wife, and were not ashamed."

Nakedness does not always bring shame. "Naked" in this verse, refers to innocent vulnerability that should be experienced in marriage. Being vulnerable emotionally, spiritually, and sexually in a marriage produces closeness and intimacy, not shame. Then, in Genesis 3:7-10 we see they were ashamed, and thus saw their nakedness. Sin exposed their hearts, motives, and actions, and therefore their nakedness.

Look at the following scriptures that show how nakedness and shame are related negatively.

- "And when Moses saw that the people were naked; (for Aaron had made them naked unto their shame among their enemies)."[5]
- "Your nakedness shall be uncovered, yes, your shame shall be seen."[6]
- "Because thou sayest, I am rich, and increased with goods, and have need of nothing; and knowest not that thou art wretched, and miserable, and poor, and blind, and naked."[7]
- "Behold, I come as a thief. Blessed is he that watcheth, and keepeth his garments, lest he walk naked, and they see his shame."[8]

Sometimes we parade our sins around just like the parades during a masquerade ball. What should be shameful, we now embrace because we are comfortable with what we are doing. "Are they ashamed of their detestable conduct? No, they have no shame at all; they do not even know how to blush. So they will fall among the fallen; they will be brought down when they are punished, says the LORD."[10] Shame came upon Adam and Eve because of their actions. But sometimes shame can come upon us because of someone else's action.

Those who have been victims of violence or abuse often feel shame. It is common for someone who feels shame due to these offenses, to cover themselves in various ways. I once heard a testimony of a women who was abused by a male family member. She remembers the negative comments he and his friends would say about "fat" woman. They would joke and say, "no one wants touch fat women." Later in life, this comment would be the very materials she would use to make her mask of shame. She intentionally gained pound after pound, in order to keep men away from her. This was the mask she was wearing. This story is not to suggest that anyone who considers themselves overweight is hiding behind a mask.

Mask #2: The Feathers of Fear

In Genesis 3:8-10, we see that the sin and shame produced fear: "Then the man and his wife heard the sound of the Lord God as he was walking in the garden in the cool of the day, and they hid from the Lord God among the trees of the garden. But the Lord God called to the man, 'Where are you?' He answered, 'I heard you in the garden, and I was afraid because I was naked; so I hid.'"[11]

Let's look at another mask. This one has feathers, and lots of them, to cover fear. Feathers on a masquerade mask are very common to cover the mask and give it volume. Fear is very common to us. What I want to drive home about this is that we all have fears such as:

> Fear of heights,
> Fear of death,
> Fear of spiders,
> Fear of snakes,
> Fear of flying,
> Fear of water,
> Fear of people,
> Fear of rejection.

Yet God said, "He did not give us a spirit of fear but power, love and a sound mind."[12] Notice in this verse "spirit of fear." Fear is something that forms in the spiritual realm. It says in Ephesians 6:12: "For we do not wrestle against flesh and blood, but against principalities, against powers, against the rulers of the darkness of this age, against spiritual hosts of wickedness in the heavenly places."[13]

When we are wearing the mask of fear, we are not allowing God to have power over the situation. We aren't operating in the love of God, and we don't have a sound mind. Instead we are powerless, fearful, and we let our imagination run away with us. A simple acronym for fear is:

False **E**vidence **A**ppearing **R**eal

False: "not real or genuine: not true or accurate; especially: deliberately untrue: done or said to fool or deceive someone: based on mistaken ideas."[14]

Evidence: "that which tends to prove or disprove something; ground for belief; proof, something that makes plain or clear; an indication or sign: law, data presented to a court or jury in proof of the facts in issue and which may include the testimony of witnesses, records, documents, or objects."[15]

Appearing: "to come into sight; become visible: to have the appearance of being; seem; look: to be obvious or easily perceived; be clear or made clear by evidence, come or be placed before the public; be published."[16]

Real: "existing or occurring as fact; actual rather than imaginary, ideal, or fictitious: being an actual thing; having objective existence; not imaginary"[1]

That spirit of fear makes us hide because we aren't sure who we are and what we are on the earth to do. We are uncertain of our purpose and the appropriate assignment for that season of our lives. We should replace this fear, uncertainty and doubt with the power of God's word, God's love and the mind of Christ.

Mask #3: Pearls of Perfection

This mask is covered with pearls. Each pearl was placed one at a time, creating a sense of unity and brilliance. "To all perfection I see a limit, but your commands are boundless."[18]

Notice a strand of real pearls. As beautiful as they all look together, not one of them is the same. Each pearl added creates a beautiful and unified piece of jewelry. The reason we will pay good money for a strand of pearls is because even though they are not all alike, there is a sense of completeness. I like to use this analogy because our efforts might look very close to being perfect, but they can't be perfect without Christ to give us unity.

Remember Adam and Eve's clothes? They thought they had a perfect solution to cover their nakedness and shame, but it took God to show them He knew what was best. Perfection doesn't leave room for God to tweak us. It doesn't leave room for us to gradually get better at our craft or develop our gifts further. It stops movement and makes us stagnant. When we strive for perfection, we can never reach it. There is always something we can do better. It leaves no room for error and leaves us feeling empty and frustrated. Being with God transforms our desire to be perfect and makes us see ourselves through His eyes. God said everything He created was good.

Mask #4: Jewels of Jealousy

The last mask I want to talk about is the mask with jewels of jealousy. Jewels are beautiful. There are many varieties of jewels. The Bible tells us that heaven has jewels. They are precious, and God refers to us as jewels. So why would I use jewels to talk about jealousy? The truth is that we wear jealousy. Just like a beautiful piece of jewelry, it is often the first thing we show. It is one of those items we pick up from time to time, and we see nothing wrong with showing it off. Jealousy can become a stronghold in our lives and destroy everything it touches. None of us look good with jealousy around our necks. It is not a badge of honor for someone to be jealous of us. When we look at someone through the eyes of this mask, we will always be deceived. We are even deceived when we look at ourselves.

Fruit from Jealousy

> Murder[19]
> Revenge-Spite[20]
> Anger and Rage[21]
> Cruelty[22]
> Hatre[23]
> Extreme Competition[24]
> Contention[25]
> Envy[26]
> Divisions[27]
> "For jealousy arouses a husband's fury..."[28]
> "Anger is cruel and fury overwhelming, but who can stand before jealousy?"[29]

Jealousy is a spirit not a jewel to show off. It causes a number of poor behavior choices and wounds many people. In Galatians, we learn about the fruit of the Spirit: "But the fruit of the Spirit is love, joy, peace, patience, kindness, goodness, faithfulness, gentleness, self-control; against such things there is no law."[30] The fruit of the spirit comes into our lives as a result of being filled with the Holy Spirit and being in God's presence. Jealousy produces the very opposite of the fruit of the Holy Spirit. Refer to the list above. I find that when someone is jealous they have a hard time focusing on God. They are always trying to see what other people are doing so they can criticize.

Jealousy puts a veil or mask over our hearts and our minds.

> "Therefore, since we have such hope, we use great boldness of speech—unlike Moses, who put a veil over his face so that the children of Israel could not look steadily at the end of what was passing away. But their minds were blinded. For until this day the same veil remains unlifted in the reading of the Old Testament, because the veil is taken away in Christ. But even to this day, when Moses is read, a veil lies on their heart. Nevertheless, when one turns to the Lord, the veil is taken away. Now the Lord is the Spirit; and where the Spirit of the Lord is, there is liberty. But we all, with unveiled face, beholding as in a mirror the glory of the Lord, are being transformed into the same image from glory to glory, just as by the Spirit of the Lord."[31]

When we know Christ, the veil over our hearts and minds is taken away, we are unmasked because we now have freedom. God is spirit and where ever He is there is freedom and liberty. Our identity comes from the very image of a spirit God. We can be transformed and unmasked as we have more knowledge about who we are relative to our purpose and our assignments. While we may feel protected by the illusions these masks provide, these illusions come at a cost; they cover the glory of God. They keep us from living in accordance of the true revelation of who God has created us to be. These complex masks of sparkly silver, feathers, pearls and jewels prevents others from seeing Christ in us.

ACTIVATION

1. So, which mask are you wearing today? Maybe, you change them daily depending on how you feel about yourself. List the mask(s) you are wearing and write down a few reasons why.

2. Maybe you are wearing a mask I did not mention. What is God showing you about the way you hide? What is He showing you about the clothes and jewelry you picked out for yourself?

ACTIVATION PRAYER

Dear Lord, show me how and why I choose to wear any mask. Let me see that You have covered me in Your love, power and I have the mind of Jesus Christ. I want to be free from sin, shame, fear, perfection, jealousy or any other mask that hides me from Your presence. Thank you for giving me courage to remove my masks. In Jesus' name, Amen!

CHAPTER 5
wounds

"For I will restore health to you and heal you of your wounds." [1]

I knew a young lady who had breast cancer several years ago. She had various treatments, and the cancer was gone after a few months. However, she still tested positive for a mutated gene which was the cause of the type of cancer she had. This gene mutation was in her bloodline. Her chances of getting cancer again, even after treatment and a clean bill of health, were over 80%, and she decided to have her breast removed and reconstructed. The cosmetic surgeons removed fat from her belly to reconstruct her breast. She came through surgery, but within a few weeks, it was obvious the tissue was not healing. In spite of the daily care and dressing of the wounds, the skin was not healing either. She was scheduled for another surgery to remove the dead tissue and insert a "wound vac."

A "vacuum-assisted closure (VAC) is a sophisticated development of a standard surgical procedure—the use of vacuum-assisted drainage to remove blood or serous fluid from a wound or operation site…The application of negative pressure in vacuum-assisted closure removes edema fluid from the wound through suction. This results in increased blood flow to the wound (by causing the blood vessels to dilate) and greater cell proliferation. Another important benefit of fluid removal is the reduction in bacterial colonization of the wound, which decreases the risk of wound infections. Through these effects, vacuum-assisted closure enhances the formation of granulation tissue, an important factor in wound healing and closure."[2]

WHAT ARE WOUNDS?

Wounds are injuries, usually involving division of tissue or rupture of the integument or mucous membrane, due to external violence or some mechanical agency rather than disease. An emotional injury does harm to our feelings, sensibility, reputation, etc.[3] Wounds often have pus and blood in them, causing them to hurt and be tender to the touch. They smell when they are infected and need daily attention. With the right medications and covering, they can heal properly. Wounds tend to heal from the inside out.

> "But He was wounded for our transgressions, He was bruised for our iniquities; the chastisement for our peace was upon Him, and by His stripes we are healed."[4]

The above scripture refers to the physical wounds and bruises Jesus endured from His public beating and crucifixion. His wounds were not only physical. He was chastised, for our peace. He was wounded emotionally. There are all kinds of wounds we receive in life. The course of the process will reveal hidden wounds and reopen some wounds so they can heal properly.

Let's talk about relationship and emotional wounds. We have all been hurt by someone—maybe a best friend, a spouse, or a sibling. Relationships can be difficult, especially when there is a lack of good communication. The deepest hurts can come from those we love. We don't always know why people hurt us. Trying to discern if we have offended them or if their painful actions were done intentionally or not, can cause confusion and pain. But that pain can turn into bitterness, resentment and anger, causing a wound.

> "Whether you've been hurt by a child, boyfriend or girlfriend, co-worker, or spouse, the Lord wants to bring restoration and healing. He can touch the deepest hurts and untangle even the most complicated relational webs, because 'with God, all things are possible.'"[5, 6]

All things, including relationships can be restored and healed by God, no matter how badly they were damaged. Emotional wounds are altogether different, even if they come from relationships. They are often inflicted at various times in our lives without there being any visible wound. Yet we are aware they are there. Wounds that are hidden deep underneath the surface of our hearts can be the most dangerous. We tend to care for what is obvious and ignore what is not seen by other.

It is important to identify emotional wounds because they are naturally hidden deep inside. They stay hidden until some form of trauma causes them to resurface. Let's look closely at a list of how emotional wounds can manifest in our personalities.

Irritability
No tolerance
Feelings of anger, hate, even resentment
Over-sensitivity
Difficulty forgiving
Doesn't feel loved
Anger towards God and others
Self-hatred
Frustration
Cutting
Retaliates and revenge
Irresponsible and destructive behavior
Unrealistic expectations of others
Perfectionism
Hopelessness
Obsessive Compulsive Disorder or OCD

Regardless of what kind of wounds you might have, each one affects the condition of the soul. The soul is the part of us that holds our mind, will, and emotions. How can the soul become wounded? According to author and speaker Katie Souza, there are two sources: sin and trauma.[7]

SIN

We most often think of sin as wrongdoing or transgression of God's law. Sin includes a failure to do what is right and offends people in its violence and lovelessness, and or course, rebellion against God. The Bible teaches that sin involves a condition in which the heart is corrupted and inclined toward evil. Our sins, no matter what they are, can cause a wound in the soul.

"As for me, I said, 'O Lord, be gracious to me; Heal my soul, for I have sinned against You.'"[8]

"Blessed [fortunate, prosperous, favored by God] is he whose transgression is forgiven, and whose sin is covered. Blessed is the man to whom the Lord does not impute wickedness, and in whose spirit there is no deceit. When I kept silent about my sin, my body wasted away, through my groaning all the day long. For day and night Your hand [of displeasure] was heavy upon me; my energy (vitality, strength) was drained away as with the burning heat of summer. Selah."[9]

"I acknowledged my sin to You, and I did not hide my wickedness; I said, "I will confess [all] my transgressions to the Lord"; and You forgave the guilt of my sin. Selah."[10]

"When I kept it all inside, my bones turned to powder, my words became daylong groans. The pressure never let up; all the juices of my life dried up. Then I let it all out; I said, 'I'll make a clean breast of my failures to God.' Suddenly the pressure was gone—my guilt dissolved, my sin disappeared."[11]

The sin of others causes wounds in the soul as well. There are many ways we can be sinned against. Being robbed could create a sense of insecurity. Being jumped by a group of people, could cause a sense of vulnerability in a crowd. Sexual, physical, or emotional abuse could cause shame and guilt. In a later chapter, I share my personal experience with an assault from a boyfriend I had in college. That experience caused me to not trust men. We should ask God to show us the wound in our soul, so He can heal it.

TRAUMA

> "Then the king swore an oath and said, 'As the Lord lives, who has redeemed my soul from all distress.'"[12]

2 Kings 4, tells a story is about a Shunamite woman who welcomed the prophet Elisha into her home to stay when he was traveling through her town. She blessed him, and he prophesied she would have a son. She gave birth to a son the next year, and he grew. The story picks up in verse 18:

> "When the child was grown, the day came that he went out to his father, to the reapers. But he said to his father, 'My head, my head.' The man said to his servant, 'Carry him to his mother.' When he had carried and brought him to his mother, he sat on her lap until noon, and then he died. She went up and laid him on the bed of the man of God, and shut the door [of the small upper room] behind him and left."[13]

> "So she set out and came to the man of God at Mount Carmel. When the man of God saw her at a distance, he said to Gehazi his servant, 'Look, there is the Shunamite woman. Please run now to meet her and ask her, 'Is it well with you? Is it well with your husband? Is it well with the child?' And she answered, 'It is well.' When she came to the mountain to the man of God, she took hold of his feet. Gehazi approached to push her away; but the man of God said, 'Let her alone, for her soul is desperate and troubled within her; and the Lord has hidden the reason from me and has not told me.' Then she said, 'Did I ask for a son from my lord? Did I not say, do not give me false hope?'"[14]

This is a story of trauma that was brought upon the house of couple who had served the prophet of the Lord; their son died. The woman went to find the prophet. As the prophet saw her coming in the distance, he knew something was wrong. He sent his servant to ask, "Is it well with you?" The servant returned with her answer and Elisha said, "let her alone, for her soul is desperate and troubled within her."

The death of a child is the worst thing that could happen to a parent. There are no words, no explanations that can calm the soul after that traumatic event. This kind of trauma overtakes the family and leaves them hopeless, often for a lifetime. I am familiar with this because my sweet niece was killed in a car accident at the age of fourteen months.

The distress, despair, and grief we felt as a family was unbearable. But the worst part of this trauma was that we watched our brother suffer, grieve, and mourn for many years. It seemed as if there was nothing any of us could do or say. We were truly lost for words and had pain beyond our comprehension. The trauma caused us to cry out to the Lord, and God brought a unity and peace to our family that only He could.

Trauma can be caused inside or outside the body. If you have had a deep cut, a broken bone, or were severally burned, you know the trauma to the body was noticeable upon impact. But it was also noticeable while it was healing. Emotional trauma is quite different and can take many years to heal, provided the process of healing is able to discover the entry point of the wound. As the prophet Elisha said above, "the Lord has hidden the reason from me and has not told me." Sometimes the matter of the heart is hidden from others.

It might seem on the outside that everything is normal, but there is something that lingers when we are hurt. Have you even seen a person and could tell they were sad? They might have been doing normal activities but something was wrong, there was a sadness in them, kind of like Hannah. We might think we are hiding our inner wounds, but soon evidence rises to the top and is noticeable by those around us. But God knows the secret: "the secret things belong to the LORD our God."[15]

> "Trauma, it affects all of us, at one point or another. Sometimes, it affects us physically, leaving behind visible scars and tangible brokenness. Other times, it comes in the form of an emotional ordeal or mental blow that devastates our hearts, infiltrates our minds, and imbeds itself in our memories. Whatever its form, trauma is a powerful experience, and its effects are far more pervasive than most people probably realize."[16]

It is important to treat a wound as soon as possible so that it does not get infected. We might use water, alcohol, or peroxide to clean it, but then use an oral or topical medicine or herb to prevent infections. An infection can be an invasion of the body by pathogenic microorganisms. Some signs of an infection are an odor, pus, and blood. This requires the infection to be covered with some type of protective layer to help the wound heal. Some types of wounds need a "wound vac." This kind of treatment was necessary in the story of the woman I shared at the beginning of the chapter. In essence, this vacuum would help the wound heal faster and eventually close it by promoting healing from the inside out. Some wounds are so deep, inner healing has to take place first. Do you need inner healing today?

When we are wounded emotionally, we go through the same process to care for a physical wound. We clean it, add some medications, and cover it so it won't become infected. Often, we wash it by erasing the memories of its existence. Not remembering is a survival mechanism when we can't handle the pain and emotions associated with the trauma. We use all kinds of distractions, such as drugs, alcohol, sex, etc. Or we may not apply medications at all because they sting. Then we cover the wound behind a smile, anger, our wealth, and other methods so no one will see it.

Wounds bring us attention. Have you ever noticed a child with a Band-Aid? If you say, "Hi," they will immediately show you their "owie." They have to show you their bandage because they want you to feel sorry for them. "Oh, what happened? How did you hurt yourself?" Adults with emotional wounds do the same thing. Our wounds will either scare observers away or make them feel sorry for us.

Self-pity can come as a result of an open wound. Self-pity is pity for oneself, especially a self-indulgent attitude concerning one's own difficulties, hardships, etc.[17] I want us to look at the fruit of self-pity. Below is a list taken from the book, *Healing the Heart of a Woman* by author Laura Gagnon.

- Shifts blame onto others.
- Is easily angered and offended; pouts.
- Sees themselves as a victim. Makes excuses and refused the redemption of Christ.
- Takes advantage of the compassion of others and manipulates their emotions so that others sympathize with them.
- Would rather complain about their problems than be healed.
- Elevates self-will rather than submission to God.
- Refuses to take responsibility of ownership of their

areas of guilt and sin. Unrepentant.
- Prefers spiritual weakness rather than strength from obedience.
- Wears people out with incessant complaining and need for attention for their issues.
- When confronted with truth, quickly changes topic of conversation. Has a knack of intimidating others and accusing them of not caring.
- Rejects true spiritual authority and embraces counterfeit authority or those that will not challenge the truth.
- Focuses on self rather than Jesus; denies the power of the cross of Christ.[18]

This is a pretty sobering list. Can you see some of these aspects of self-pity in your life? Well, the truth is, we have all fallen into this trap at some point. When wounds dig deep into our souls, they produce unsettling behavior patterns.

DANGER IN OPEN WOUNDS

When we are wounded emotionally, we speak from our wounds. Our conversations are about our wounds. Our focus, consciously and subconsciously, is always on our wounds. We need to be careful not to help others from of our wounds. For when we speak and try to give others advice from our wounds, we do so through our blood, pus, and pain!

Listen very carefully: we can't help someone heal from a wound if we haven't seen and experienced the healing first hand. The wound is still tender and needs the proper attention to heal, or it will get worse. We tend to group ourselves with people who have the same wound, so no one gets better, no one heals. Sure, we can relate to them, we cry with them and identify with them. But we never get better from them, and they don't get better from us. Jesus is our Healer, and it is His blood that should cover our sins. Let's go to Jesus to heal our wounds, so we can point others to Jesus and not ourselves.

WOUNDS ISOLATE

Our wounds can cause us to be isolated. People often respond to wounds negatively, and there isn't always the compassion we are looking and hoping for. Let's look at the incurable disease of leprosy in the Bible.

Leprosy was repulsive and incurable. Everyone who had this disease was cast outside of the city limits. Often, Lepers would form communities because they did not have access to the resources in the cities. They were not allowed to have physical contact with anyone other than other Lepers or the priest once they were clean.

Leviticus 13 and 14 contain the laws concerning leprosy. The priest was in charge of the process of confirming whether a person had leprosy. They first had to examine the skin, hair, and sores present, and then pronounce them unclean: "The priest shall examine the sore on the skin of the body; and if the hair on the sore has turned white, and the sore appears to be deeper than the skin of his body, it is a leprous sore. Then the priest shall examine him, and pronounce him unclean."[19]

A process of isolation gave the priest the opportunity to watch the progression of the sores and reexamine the individual: "But if the bright spot is white on the skin of his body, and does not appear to be deeper than the skin, and its hair has not turned white, then the priest shall isolate the one who has the sore seven days."[20]

the process

> "Now the leper on whom the sore is, his clothes shall be torn and his head bare; and he shall cover his mustache, and cry, 'Unclean! Unclean!' He shall be unclean. All the days he has the sore he shall be unclean. He is unclean, and he shall dwell alone; his dwelling shall be outside the camp."[21]

The priest pronounced the person clean or unclean based on several criteria.

> "But when raw flesh appears on him, he shall be unclean. And the priest shall examine the raw flesh and pronounce him to be unclean; for the raw flesh is unclean. It is leprosy. Or if the raw flesh changes and turns white again, he shall come to the priest. And the priest shall examine him; and indeed if the sore has turned white, then the priest shall pronounce him clean who has the sore. He is clean."[22]

The process for cleansing the leper was very involved. The priest had to examine the leper and pronounce them clean. An offering was made; the person was to wash in water, shave their hair, beard and eyebrows, and wash his clothes in water. They were to live outside the city for several days and then make another sacrifice, be presented to the priest, followed by more sacrifices, and other customs following that.

The Levitical law set in place many rules for the health and safety of the people. The process by which the laws were carried created structure in the community. We also have laws in our current society. They may not be as involved as those we read from the book of Leviticus, but they are just as important. These laws are there to keep the community at large safe.

Many of us will never see a person with leprosy unless we google it on the internet. We may never know the physical and emotional pain a victim of leprosy faces. In the Old Testament, the wounds of a leper caused him to be separated from his family, shunned by his community, and completely isolated until he was clean or had died. Today, you might feel like one of these lepers. Your physical wounds might cause a separation. Your emotional wounds might cause shame and guilt. But Jesus has compassion for you and wants to make you clean, well, and whole.

> "Now a leper came to Him, imploring Him, kneeling down to Him and saying to Him, 'If You are willing, You can make me clean.' Then Jesus, moved with compassion, stretched out His hand and touched him, and said to him, 'I am willing; be cleansed.' As soon as He had spoken, immediately the leprosy left him, and he was cleansed. And He strictly warned him and sent him away at once, and said to him, 'See that you say nothing to anyone; but go your way, show yourself to the priest, and offer for your cleansing those things which Moses commanded, as a testimony to them.'"[23]

DOES TIME HEAL WOUNDS?

"'Time heals all wounds' is a myth. No, it doesn't. Forgiveness is what allows people to heal. Offense creates more offense and these that carry unhealed wounds end up hurting others. Regardless of the reasons why people incur emotional wounds, the important thing is that we each surrender our hurts to the one that can heal us."[24]

> "If My people who are called by My name will humble themselves, and pray and seek My face, and turn from their

wicked ways, then I will hear from heaven, and will forgive their sin and heal their land. Now My eyes will be open and My ears attentive to prayer made in this place. For now, I have chosen and sanctified this house, that My name may be there forever; and My eyes and My heart will be there perpetually."[25]

When we forgive, we give someone a gift and waive a penalty. We also can have grudge-free living. When we do not forgive, we not only refuse to offer what God has given to us, but we also hurt ourselves. Unforgiveness causes the heart to be heavy and stunts our spiritual growth. God knows it's not easy to forgive. But He knows it is necessary for us to heal completely. Forgiveness works a lot like a "wound vac," healing from the inside out. We can forgive because of God's grace, after all we have been forgiven through grace. Forgiveness is essential in the healing process.

Jesus spoke these words from the cross while the Roman soldiers divided His garments and cast lots.[26] This was the main reason Jesus entered the world—to redeem it, to save us from our sins, and to forgive us.[27] God did this because He loves us. Jesus Christ came supernaturally to do the supernatural and forgive mankind for our sins, past, present, and future. This type of forgiveness makes it possible for us to forgive one another. There is no other way, because it is unnatural to forgive. Christ made it possible through His blood atonement sacrifice for our sins and showed us how to forgive. Those three powerful words ("Father, forgive them") were followed soon afterwards with, "It is finished"—another set of words from Jesus that would change history forever! Christ's mission was accomplished![28]

Blessings of Forgiveness:

- Forgiveness from others.
- Forgiveness from God.
- Freedom from demonic torment.
- Freedom from focusing on our past offenses, allowing us to live for today.
- Relinquishing the anger toward the other person.
- Knowing you've done what God has asked you to do.
- Releasing of God's divine healing power—the more awful the offense, the more you need this.
- Decrease in self-condemnation.
- Releasing of thankfulness so you can live with the conscious knowledge of God's protection and love.

ACTIVATION

1. Ask God for forgiveness of your sins. Ask God to forgive you for all those you have wounded. Forgive all who have wounded you.

2. Forgiveness is a process and it will take time for the wound to heal. If you need to talk to the person or persons who have hurt you, pray about how to approach them, when and what to say.

ACTIVATION PRAYER

Father God, I thank you for the work of the cross that covers my sins. I thank you that You sent Your son, Jesus, as a sacrifice for my sin and the sins of the world. I come to You with a humble heart and ask for You to forgive me of my sins, those I am aware of and those I am not. I make the decision to forgive all those who have hurt me in any way. I pray that when I am reminded of those hurts and wounds, You will remind me of your unconditional love for me and those people. I give You permission to show me my puncture wounds and bring healing that will last a lifetime. I surrender to You daily, and I choose to abide in Your love, forgiveness, and mercy. In Jesus' name, Amen.

CHAPTER 6
issues

We all have issues, concerns, problems, and even controversy in life. These issues can be health, relationship, or financially related. There seems to be very few moments in our lives that we do not have an issue to deal with. At times, these issues come up out of nowhere, and we have to deal with them immediately, disturbing our flow. Other times we have them around and they seem to linger with no end in sight. Issues can lead to great heartache, worry, and pain. They can cause confusion and disillusion with the future. But if we look at them as a vehicle to understanding what we are going through, then we can begin to see them as a way to change our mindset and perspective on life.

In Mark 5, Matthew 9, and Luke 8, we see an account of several issues in the towns that Jesus was visiting. I am going to use the text from Mark 5:25-43 to tell the story:

"Now when Jesus had crossed over again by boat to the other side, a great multitude gathered to Him; and He was by the sea. And behold, one of the rulers of the synagogue came, Jairus by name. And when he saw Him, he fell at His feet and begged Him earnestly, saying, 'My little daughter lies at the point of death. Come and lay Your hands on her, that she may be healed, and she will live.' So Jesus went with him, and a great multitude followed Him and thronged Him.

Now a certain woman had a flow of blood for twelve years, and had suffered many things from many physicians. She had spent all that she had and was no better, but rather grew worse. When she heard about Jesus, she came behind Him in the crowd and touched His garment. For she said, 'If only I may touch His clothes, I shall be made well.'"

We see in this chapter several overlapping issues. There is Jairus' daughter, a thronging crowd, and the woman with the issue of blood flow. We should never think that our issues are more important than the issues of those around us.

ISSUE #1

Jairus was a well-known religious ruler in his synagogue. He was privileged in many ways. As a leader, he could access the best doctors and advice, but his daughter was dying. Because of the humbled posture of his plea, this issue must have happened very suddenly. The scripture doesn't say when he left his house to go get help or that he was even looking for Jesus. But it seemed Jairus knew that if Jesus would come to his house and lay hands on his daughter, she would recover.

When Jairus saw Jesus in the crowd, he did what he could to get his attention. He begged and fell at his feet, a sign of humility and respect. He invited Jesus to come, lay hands on and heal his dying daughter. He believed in the touch of Jesus and His ability to heal. His desperate plea was acknowledged by Jesus, and He went with him. Jairus was going to Jesus on behalf of his daughter, he was clearly worried and concerned. How many times do our issues involve other people? We might be directly involved, or we might be a bystander, but we are still affected by the circumstances.

ISSUE #2

The scripture said, "the multitude thronged him." To throng is "to crowd into; fill: to press against in large numbers: to gather, press, or move in a throng."[1] The crowd was pressing in, trying to get to Jesus. Some in the crowd thronged Him because they had personal issues to deal with. Others thronged Him because they wanted a closer look at the man everyone was talking about. And yet others were mocking and creating a commotion in the crowd.

This thronging crowd held Jesus up and made it difficult to move with ease to his destination, Jairus' house. I'm sure for Jairus the crowd was annoying, and there was panic in his heart. Every step Jesus took must have seemed like an eternity for Jairus and the grieving family. But the thronging crowd held Jesus up long enough for a certain woman to touch Him.

ISSUE #3

The scripture above states, "Now a certain woman had a flow of blood for twelve years." She is referred to in other Bible versions as the "woman with the issue of blood." We are told this woman spent all the money she had to get help from the doctors and yet she was still very sick. She had heard of Jesus, and when she saw He was near, she joined in the throng of people following Him as He made His way to Jairus' house.

"For she said, 'If only I may touch His clothes, I shall be made well.'" This woman was going to Jesus because she had a personal issue that had affected her finances as well as her relationships. She was physically ill and for twelve years, with a flow of blood, draining her energy and depleting her body of nutrients. Everyone in the town knew her and knew she was unclean because she was forced to shout, "unclean" to announce her appearance. People would look around to find the voice that shouted "unclean." They would cover their faces, grab their children, and create as much distance between themselves and her as they could. They did not even know what her issue was, and no one would ever stop to ask.

> "Jewish Law declared her to be ceremonially unclean due to her bleeding issue. This meant that she would not have been permitted to enter the temple for Jewish religious ceremonies. According to the Law, anything or anyone she touched became unclean as well. The fact that she was in the crowd pressing around Jesus means that each person who bumped into her would have become unclean, too—including Jesus."[2]

> "If a woman has a discharge of blood for many days, other than at the time of her customary impurity, or if it runs beyond her usual time of impurity, all the days of her unclean discharge shall be as the days of her customary impurity. She shall be unclean. Every bed on which she lies all the days of her discharge shall be to her as the bed of her impurity; and whatever she sits on shall be unclean,

as the uncleanness of her impurity. Whoever touches those things shall be unclean; he shall wash his clothes and bathe in water, and be unclean until evening."[3]

UNCLEAN, UNCLEAN

She was ceremonially unclean because of the bleeding. Can you imagine being this woman? The cause of her bleeding could have been from many sources, including a uterine fibroid, which is a benign tumor. These tumors can be different sizes and may be located inside or out of the uterus. There can be one or many. There are many problems associated with fibroids, including bleeding, pain, pressure, and an enlarged stomach. I have known many women who have had fibroids in their uterus that causes constant bleeding. It is a common condition. There are medical ways to remove them today. One is to remove the tumor from the uterus. Another way to remove the entire uterus because there are multiple fibroids. Her issue wasn't going to go away by putting on protective clothing under her garments to absorb the flow; she was unable to hide it or her shame. She was customarily impure for twelve long years. Her whole life was disrupted.

The Bible doesn't say, but what if she had been married? This would have affected her time of intimacy with her husband because the blood flow lasted so long. There is also the possibility she would have been divorced or cast away. She wasn't able to hug her children, cook for them, and be near them without causing them to suffer the same humiliation she had. Her issue had a ripple effect and caused her to be isolated and rejected.

The woman's issue was private, yet she had to deal with the opinions, concerns, and scrutiny of others. Many women have this condition today and yet they are not scrutinized. They simply deal with it privately and have the freedom to go to a doctor of their choice for help. "For she said, 'If only I may touch His clothes, I shall be made well.'" She went for it, pressed through the crowd, and touched Him. She touched Jesus—what faith!

> "Immediately the fountain of her blood was dried up, and she felt in her body that she was healed of the affliction. And Jesus, immediately knowing in Himself that power had gone out of Him, turned around in the crowd and said, 'Who touched My clothes?' But His disciples said to Him, 'You see the multitude thronging You, and You say, 'Who touched Me?'' And He looked around to see her who had done this thing. But the woman, fearing and trembling, knowing what had happened to her, came and fell down before Him and told Him the whole truth. And He said to her, 'Daughter, your faith has made you well. Go in peace, and be healed of your affliction.'"[4]

She was healed even in the midst of the thronging crowd, and Jesus knew it. "Who touched me?" Jesus knows when we have touched Him. He never ignores us. We might not get an immediate response, but He knows. Verse 32 is my favorite: "And He looked around to see her who had done this thing." Jesus was looking for her, and He is looking for you. Don't run and hide. Don't cover your face and say, "never mind." Jesus is searching for you because you have touched Him with your prayers, your tears, your pleas, and your faith.

The woman fell to the ground out of fear. Remember she was unclean and was not supposed to be out of her restricted area without shouting "unclean." Everything she touched was considered unclean, except Jesus, or course. Her faith made her well.

JAIRUS

Do you think Jairus cared that this common, unclean woman was healed? He was a ruler and in good standing with the law. He was allowed to be in public. Most likely he did not experience the same wonder and joy that she did; he was just trying to get his issue resolved. He needed to get Jesus through the crowd and to his house. Can you see the torment on Jairus' face? With each delay was a loss of hope. His family had already begun to mourn for the girl. "While He was still speaking, some came from the ruler of the synagogue's house who said, 'Your daughter is dead. Why trouble the Teacher any further?'"[5]

I can only imagine the despair that went through Jairus' heart when he heard those words, "Your daughter is dead." He must have experienced instant numbing and confusion. He must have wondered, if only Jesus could have arrived sooner; if only that annoying crowd would have let Him pass; if only that unclean women would have stayed in her place.

I have had many "if only" moments in my head when the outcome of the situation wasn't what I wanted nor expected. "If only" I had waited. "If only" I had listened to my dad. "If only" I had paid more attention. It is easy to get caught up in what did not happen. The "if only" sounded louder with each disappointment. "As soon as Jesus heard the word that was spoken, He said to the ruler of the synagogue, 'Do not be afraid; only believe.'"[6]

Jairus must have taken a deep breath, hearing the peace in Jesus' voice. He kept walking, still uncertain of the outcome, but hopeful because he was leading Jesus to his house. Jesus, on the other hand, did not give up on the little girl, and He didn't appear to be worried about the report. He was headed there to heal her, and on the way, someone else was healed. The healing of the certain woman wasn't going to change the healing of the dying girl. Her healing wasn't contingent upon getting to Jairus' house faster. We often think "more for someone else" means "less for us," which makes it hard for us to rejoice and be happy for others when something good happens to them.

Your friend's new husband doesn't mean you won't get married. The neighbor's pregnancy doesn't mean you won't get pregnant. His new job doesn't mean you can't have a new one, too. There is plenty of God to go around. He will supply all of our needs according to His riches in glory, not according to our thoughts or timing. Jesus told Jairus, "Do not be afraid; only believe." Jesus is also saying to you, "Do not be afraid; only believe." That dead issue in your life will come alive.

Jesus says to the family, "Why make this commotion and weep? The child is not dead, but sleeping." Sometimes the news seems far worse than the reality. We can't always make a clear-cut decision based on what we hear. We must search for more truth in the matter and listen to what God has to say. We must listen to Jesus, "Do not be afraid; only believe," rather than those people in the room who don't know what Jesus knows. "And they ridiculed Him. But when He had put them all outside, He took the father and the mother of the child, and those who were with Him, and entered where the child was lying."[7]

Jesus got rid of everyone who was not on the same page as Him, and everyone who ridiculed or had something negative to say. Not everyone around you can help with your issue. Unfortunately, others may make the matter worse. It is important to surround yourself with those who are like-minded in faith. The prayer of agreement is powerful because it moves Jesus to action. Be careful who you invite to pray with you.

> "Then He took the child by the hand, and said to her, 'Talitha, cumi,' which is translated, 'Little girl, I say to you, arise.' Immediately the girl arose and walked, for she was twelve years of age. And they were overcome with great amazement. But He commanded them strictly that no one should know it, and said that something should be given her to eat."[8]

There was another touch, but this time it was Jesus who grabbed the hand of the child and said, "Little girl, I say to you, arise." Awe and excitement filled the room as the little girl got up perfectly well. The people in your room should be excited for you when you "arise." There should be a sound of praise and "great amazement" when your issue is resolved. When you are on death's bed, is there someone who can press into the crowd and find Jesus for you? When you are afraid to press through the crowd, for fear of humiliation, Jesus is not too far away. He is only an arm's length away from your miracle.

This passage explains God's timing in this story:

> "When Jesus stopped on His way to Jairus' house to speak to the woman in the crowd, He allowed time to pass. Jesus was not worried about Jairus' daughter dying. He knew all along that He would heal her, even if that meant raising her from the dead. In a beautiful act of mercy, Jesus stops to care for the woman in the crowd who had reached out to Him in faith. Jairus undoubtedly felt the urgency of his situation, and he probably chafed at what he saw as a delay. His daughter was lying at death's door, and Jesus was taking His time. Jairus learned that God's timing and purpose are not like ours. Sometimes He requires patience from us, sometimes He waits longer than we think is rational, and

sometimes He allows temporary loss in order to show us the eternal abundance of His blessing."[9]

What did Jairus and the woman have in common? Well, it was not their personal issues. It did not appear they had any affiliation with each other. They were in the same thronging crowd, trying to reach Jesus. It was the atmosphere! They were both in the presence of Jesus and His presence caused them to press. It is time that was recognize when Jesus is in town. Could it be that God uses our issues to draw us to Him? Could it be that God is asking you to find His son Jesus, and press into Him?

Stop for a minute and stretch your arms to Jesus. Can you feel His presence? Just wait one minute. Now by faith, touch Him and be made "well." When He turns around and looks at you, notice the flow of never-ending issues dry up in that moment. Watch the dead issues in your life "arise."

MORE TO BE HEALED

If you continue to read the account in Matthew 9, you will find that beginning in verse 27 there were two blind men: "When Jesus departed from there, two blind men followed Him, crying out and saying, 'Son of David, have mercy on us!'"[10] There was also a mute and demon-possessed man: "As they went out, behold, they brought to Him a man, mute and demon-possessed."[11]

There were more issues to deal with. Jesus never stopped helping people along the way. You might think your issue is the only one that matters at the time, and you might think no one cares that you are suffering. You might think that there is little or no relief or solution in sight. You might think you are stuck. If you would just fall on your knees, like Jairus; if you would push through the crowd and reach out and touch Him, like the certain woman; if you would cry out, like the blind men, you would find that even when you can't speak for yourself, Jesus is on the way and He will heal you.

THE COMPASSION OF JESUS

> "Then Jesus went about all the cities and villages, teaching in their synagogues, preaching the gospel of the kingdom, and healing every sickness and every disease among the people. But when He saw the multitudes, He was moved with compassion for them, because they were weary and scattered, like sheep having no shepherd. Then He said to His disciples, 'The harvest truly is plentiful, but the laborers are few. Therefore, pray the Lord of the harvest to send out laborers into His harvest.'"[12]

You see, Jesus was moved with compassion and healed "every sickness and every disease." He is moved with compassion for you and will heal every sickness (physical, mental, emotional, relational) and every disease. Where is your sickness? Where is your dis-ease? Jesus is in your town, and is walking in the thronging crowd. He is moved with compassion, so don't keep silent when He passes by. Get in the press.

Are you desperate enough to push through the crowd? Will you break the social taboos? Will you be willing to look silly in front of others? When you hear Jesus is near, do you join the crowd and press and throng? Are you willing to get close enough to touch Him?

ACTIVATION

1. What are the issues that need to be addressed in your life? They might be personal, family related, or church and community related. Write them down.

2. Jesus said to His disciples to pray for laborers for the harvest of people. He knew there were others who had His compassion to help those in need. Maybe today you aren't needing an issue resolved, but you know that others need help. Ask God to give you compassion for those around you, and ask Him to show you what to do.

ACTIVATION PRAYER

Dear Lord, I thank you that You know all my issues. You are aware of those issues I cannot speak about for fear I will be judged. I am unclean in many ways. But Lord, I ask You to make me clean. I ask You to look at my cry and petition for these circumstances. Thank you for having compassion for me and that I am not alone during this time. I stretch my hands to You, in faith that I am healed of all my infirmities. Heal every part of me. May the peace of God which surpasses all of my understanding guard my heart and mind in Christ Jesus, Amen!

CHAPTER 7
unseen war

Throughout history, there have been many wars in countries and regions around the world. Wars may be between ethnic groups, or they may be civil wars, social and economic wars, wars for control and occupation, and wars between family members. We live with the threat daily, and there are more wars to come in the future. The loss of life, land, freedom, and safety threaten our national and international peace. Most of us will never go to war. We won't have to fight in the armed services for our country. Most will never go to a foreign land and battle for the protection and rights of others. But those who have fought throughout history are aware of the great price of war. The cost of war has devastating implications. It seems as if neither side is a winner, although there is a declared victory. We live on earth, and the reality of war is all around us.

the process

We are at war with an invisible enemy. I don't mean a specific country or ethnic group, but a war with an unseen army in the spiritual realm. All Christians are called to war, and if you understand the war and your authority in Christ, you will not be afraid.

There is a spiritual war that has been going on before the foundations of the earth. We see the evidence of this war when a loved one is addicted to drugs, or when there is sexual sin, pride, depression, fear or jealousy. We see the manifestations of this spiritual war when someone is murdered, or a baby is aborted. But how are these manifestation, how are these specific problems evidence of war? That is what we are going to explore in this chapter.

THE WAR IN HEAVEN

> "God's Message came to me: 'Son of man, raise a funeral song over the King of Tyre. Tell him, A Message from God, the Master':
>
> > 'You had everything going for you.
> > You were in Eden, God's garden.
> > You were dressed in splendor,
> > your robe studded with jewels:
> > Carnelian, peridot, and moonstone,
> > beryl, onyx, and jasper,
> > Sapphire, turquoise, and emerald,
> > all in settings of engraved gold.
> > A robe was prepared for you
> > the same day you were created.
> > You were the anointed cherub.
> > I placed you on the mountain of God.

You strolled in magnificence
among the stones of fire.
From the day of your creation
you were sheer perfection
 and then imperfection—evil! —was detected in you.
In much buying and selling
you turned violent, you sinned!
I threw you, disgraced, off the mountain of God.
I threw you out—you, the anointed angel-cherub.
No more strolling among the gems of fire for you!
Your beauty went to your head.
You corrupted wisdom
by using it to get worldly fame.
I threw you to the ground,
sent you sprawling before an audience of kings
and let them gloat over your demise.
By sin after sin after sin,
by your corrupt ways of doing business,
you defiled your holy places of worship.
So I set a fire around and within you.
It burned you up. I reduced you to ashes.
All anyone sees now
they look for you is ashes,
a pitiful mound of ashes.
All who once knew you
now throw up their hands:
'This can't have happened!'
This has happened!'"[1]

THE FALL OF LUCIFER

> "How you are fallen from heaven,
> O Lucifer, son of the morning!
> How you are cut down to the ground,
> You who weakened the nations!
> For you have said in your heart:
> 'I will ascend into heaven,
> I will exalt my throne above the stars of God;
> I will also sit on the mount of the congregation
> On the farthest sides of the north;
> I will ascend above the heights of the clouds,
> I will be like the Most High.'
> Yet you shall be brought down to Sheol,
> To the lowest depths of the Pit.
> "Those who see you will gaze at you,
> And consider you, saying:
> 'Is this the man who made the earth tremble,
> Who shook kingdoms,
> Who made the world as a wilderness
> And destroyed its cities,
> Who did not open the house of his prisoners?'"[2]

These two scriptures are the account of the fall of Lucifer, also known as Satan. "How you have fallen from heaven, O morning star, son of the dawn! You have been cast down to the earth, you who once laid low the nations!" Jesus said, "I saw Satan fall like lightning from heaven,"[3] and in the book of Revelation, Satan is seen as "a star that had fallen from the sky to the earth."[4]

Lucifer was an angel who rebelled against God, coveted the throne of God and the worship which belonged to God alone. This resulted in a mighty war in heaven. Lucifer, along with one third of the angelic host, were cast down from heaven to the earth, where he became known as "Satan," a name which literally means "Adversary" as well as "Devil,"[5] or "Accuser of the brethren."[6]

> "Angels are personal spiritual beings who have intelligence, emotions, and will. This is true of both the good and evil angels (demons). Angels possess intelligence,[7] show emotion,[8] and exercise will (Luke 8:28-31; 2 Timothy 2:26; Jude 6).[9] Angels are spirit beings without true physical bodies.[10] Although they do not have physical bodies, they are still personalities."[11]

God has a heavenly army of angels at His command. He is "Lord of hosts," a title that occurs often in the Old Testament. In Hebrew, God is called Yahweh Sabaoth, meaning "Lord of the heavenly armies" or "God of the heavenly hosts." God is fully capable of fighting for us.

> "Lift up your heads, O gates!
> And be lifted up, O ancient doors,
> that the King of glory may come in.
> Who is this King of glory?
> The Lord, strong and mighty,
> the Lord, mighty in battle!
> Lift up your heads, O gates!
> And lift them up, O ancient doors,
> that the King of glory may come in.
> Who is this King of glory?
> The Lord of hosts,
> he is the King of glory! Selah."[12]

the process

God is the King of glory, and He is also a warrior who is strong and mighty. He is the great commander of the heavenly army, "The Lord of Hosts." The process of war requires a commander, as well as, a well-trained military to carry out various tactics. A commander is challenged with the task of creating a plan, strategic moves, and preparing the army for a victory. He needs to be aware of the enemy, its tactics, and where the enemy is located.

WHERE IS THE WAR?

> "Finally, my brethren, be strong in the Lord and in the power of His might. Put on the whole armor of God, that you may be able to stand against the wiles of the devil. For we do not wrestle against flesh and blood, but against principalities, against powers, against the rulers of the darkness of this age, against spiritual hosts of wickedness in the heavenly places. Therefore, take up the whole armor of God, that you may be able to withstand in the evil day, and having done all, to stand."[13]

Remember Psalm 24: "Who is this King of glory? The Lord, strong and mighty, the Lord, mighty in battle!" Ephesians 6:11 says, "Be strong in the Lord and in the power of His might." We are not to go to war without God, our commander, and we are not to fight in our own might. Our war is not a natural war. We are not fighting people and countries; the Bible clearly tells us we are fighting a war against the army of hell, with Satan as its commander. Yes, the war is against Satan and his army in heavenly places, the unseen world. Satan has always been after God's throne and everything that belongs to Him. So, he is also after us. We are the sons and daughter of a great and mighty king, The Lord of Hosts.

Ron Phillips' article on spiritual warfare was featured in the *Spiritual Warfare Bible*, called "The Army of Hell."[14] In it he gives a description of the invisible enemies taught about in Ephesians 6: Principalities, powers, rulers of the darkness and spiritual hosts of wickedness. Read more about spiritual warfare in Ron's book, "Everyone's Guide to Demons and Spiritual Warfare."

Principalities

"Top-ranking demonic beings are called principalities. The word *principalities* is translated from the Greek word *arche*, which means 'chief.' These are the chief demons, which correspond with the archangels among the holy angels. The apostle Paul wrote that these princes hold sway over the souls of people.[14] A principality is what assigns demonic spirits to operate in the disobedient. Also, these princes rule over continents and nations. In Daniel 10:12-12 the prophet is informed by Gabriel (an angel) that a principality of Persia had hindered his arrival to Daniel for three weeks. Gabriel had to summon the archangel Michael to take on the arch-devil of Persia."

Powers

"The next rank of evil officers of darkness is called 'powers.' The word *powers* comes from the Greek word *exousia*, which means 'delegated authority,' like that of a policeman. These demons seem to operate invisibly in governmental centers such as nation governments."

Rulers of The Darkness

"The next level of demonic leaders touches the created order. 'Rulers of the darkness' is translated from Greek word *kosmokrator*, which means "to seize and take hold of governments for the sake of darkness and evil. Kosmas had to do with 'an arrangement or order.' These rulers want to take over the offices of government, the legislatures, and the courts."

Spiritual Forces of Wickedness

"Spiritual host of wickedness literally means in the Greek 'spiritual fakes.' The word wicked is *poneria*, from which we get fornication and pornography. These are the unclean spirits we deal with on a daily basis. Some of these spirits are named for us. Beelzebub means 'lord of the flies.' Abaddon, or Apollyon, means 'Destroyer.' Damon means 'torment the mind' These lower-level spirits are the ones we deal with daily. Satan's army is well organized, and his legions employ an array of methods and schemes. We must be prepared to face down this infernal enemy and expose his tactics.

I want you to read this passage of scriptures in a couple of other translations:

"A final word: Be strong in the Lord and in his mighty power. Put on all of God's armor so that you will be able to stand firm against all strategies of the devil. For we are not fighting against flesh-and-blood enemies, but against evil rulers and authorities of the unseen world, against mighty powers in this dark world, and against evil spirits in the heavenly places."[15]

"And that about wraps it up. God is strong, and He wants you strong. So take everything the Master has set out for you, well-made weapons of the best materials. And put them to use so you will be able to stand up to everything the Devil throws your way. This is no afternoon athletic contest that we'll walk away from and forget about in a couple of hours. This is for keeps, a life-or-death fight to the finish against the Devil and all his angels."[16]

God wants us prepared for the battle. We have an enemy that wants to destroy us. God is fully aware and He prepares us for the war by exposing the enemy and giving us armor. Ephesians 6:13-18 is a powerful scripture full of wisdom and insight. I would encourage you to know it well and refer to it often, especially when you find yourself in a difficult situation or relationship. It will give you a new perspective on who you are fighting and how to win the battle.

It is not enough to have the knowledge of a war that none of us really want to fight. We must know who to fight, and we must be prepared. Equipped soldiers understand the armor and weapons that have been issued to them. We have been given help to have confidence that we are on the winning team. No weapon that is formed or used by the enemy against us will prosper, succeed, flourish, or rule over us.

ARMOR AND WEAPONS

1. Belt of truth: Jesus is the way the truth and the life.[17] You will know the truth and the truth will set you free.[18] The truth is against the lies of Satan, the "father of lies."[19]

2. Breastplate of righteousness: A breastplate is a protective cover that protects the vital organs such as the heart and lungs. Righteousness refers to the righteousness of Christ. "Above all else, guard your heart, for everything you do flows from it."[20]

3. Shoes of peace: As we are at war and walk on the terrain of the enemy, we need to protect our feet. Jesus is the King of Peace.[21]

4. Shield of faith: The shield quenches the "fiery arrows of the enemy." The enemy is always going against what God said. Jesus is the author and finisher of our faith.[22] The shield goes in front of us, before the body. The Lord God is the sun and shield He gives grace and glory.[23]

5. Helmet of salvation: We should guard our hearts and minds in Christ Jesus. The battle often starts in the mind. That is where the enemy loves to get us to doubt God. When our minds are in partnership of Jesus, through salvation we can stand against false doctrine, lies and we won't give way to Satan's temptations. Salvation is crucial to using these weapons. Without it we are defenseless and incapable of discerning between spiritual truth and spiritual deception. Let this mind which is in Christ Jesus also be in me.[24] I have the mind of Christ.[25]

6. Sword of the Spirit, "God's Word": The Holy Spirit gives us power. He has a weapon of choice, "The word of God." If that is His weapon and He is the spirit of God, how much more do we need to know and stand on the word of God. We will not live by bread alone

but every word that proceeds from the mouth of God.[26] When Jesus was tempted in the desert, He used the Word of God to fight Satan. The word was His sword.

7. Prayer: Prayer is a weapon. It is how we access God who is also spirit in the spiritual realm. "In verse 18, we are told to pray in the Spirit (that is, with the mind of Christ, with His heart and His priorities) in addition to wearing the full armor of God. We cannot neglect prayer, as it is the means by which we draw spiritual strength from God. Without prayer, without reliance upon God, our efforts at spiritual warfare are empty and futile. The full armor of God—truth, righteousness, the gospel, faith, salvation, the Word of God, and prayer—are the tools God has given us, through which we can be spiritually victorious, overcoming Satan's attacks and temptations."[27]

8. Watch: We have to watch where we are because Satan walks around like a lion seeking for a chance to devour us.[28] Many Christians walk around completely oblivious to what is going on around them.

In the process of war, you will find yourself in many battles with the unseen enemy. Remember, the enemy may be unseen, but he manifests himself in works and behaviors that we consider to be a normal part of our society. We are affected in so many negative ways from our sin and the sin of others. Often, though, we don't acknowledge where these attacks are coming from. It seems as if we don't always want to know. It makes us less fearful when we diminish the existence of Satan and his schemes. But in reality, we are always under attack. I don't know about you, but I want to stop the attacks on me and my family. I am going to use the armor and weapons that God gave me to defeat him. In the next chapter, I am going to expose some of the undercover spirits (demons) that are working to keep you from understanding your identity, holding you to your past, and preventing you from walking in your purpose.

ACTIVATION

Put your armor on each morning. Stand up and physically put the armor on as if you were putting on clothes.

ACTIVATION PRAYER

Dear Lord, I am so thankful You gave me insight into the battle that I face each day. I thank you for exposing the enemy's tactics and location. Right now, I choose to put on the full armor You gave me in Your word. I start by putting on my belt of truth so I can seek and know Your truth in all situations. I place the Breastplate of Righteousness on to my chest to guard my heart. I place my shoes of the gospel of peace, on each foot so, I can walk in peace knowing You are my peace. I take the shield of faith in my hand so I can withstand the arrows and darts the enemy would send my way. My helmet of salvation is secure because it protects my mind, thoughts and intellect from being trapped in the world's mindset. I grab the sword of the spirit which is double-edged because it is the word of God. I am ready for battle, in Jesus' name.

CHAPTER 8
strongholds

"For the weapons of our warfare are not carnal but mighty in God for pulling down strongholds, casting down arguments and every high thing that exalts itself against the knowledge of God, bringing every thought into captivity to the obedience of Christ, and being ready to punish all disobedience when your obedience is fulfilled."[1]

STRONGHOLDS CAN DELAY THE PROCESS

God did not leave us to fend for ourselves; He provided armor and weapons that destroy the enemy's camp and strongholds. A stronghold is "a well-fortified place; fortress, a place that serves as the center of a group, as of militants or of persons holding a controversial viewpoint."[2] As we see in the definition, strongholds can be physical or mental. They can be fortified by a group of people or one person. According to author and speaker, Kimberly Daniels, a "stronghold is a spiritual place of bondage. Physical places can become spiritual strongholds, or a person can simply be garrisoned in their mind."³

Strongholds affect our minds. They penetrate our thought process and enter our hearts. They are lies and deceptions based on past experience, trauma, the way we were raised, our environment, our generational bloodline, and other factors. Once strongholds get a "strong," (mentally powerful or vigorous)⁴ "hold" (to remain fast; adhere; cling: to keep or maintain a grasp on something. to maintain one's position against opposition; continue in resistance),⁵ they begin to shape and form our life's philosophy and belief systems. They become the guide for making decisions. They become the standard for relationships. They become the voice we are conditioned to hearing.

Once we have our armor on, we can advance into the battlefield. There is no stronghold of the enemy that will not come down. Notice the scripture says, "pulling down" strongholds, "casting down" arguments and every "high thing that exalts" itself. Remember the war is in the heavenly places and not on earth. We are not fighting people, i.e. our parents, husbands, wives, children, boss, or the church, but the spiritual and emotional mindset presented by Satan and acted out by people. The direction we are moving Satan's kingdom is always down. We are casting it down because he tries to exalt himself and his kingdom above God's kingdom. This particular scripture also exposes where the enemy tries to set up strongholds-in "arguments, vain imagination and "proud obstacles." Arguments, vain imaginations and pride are often found in our opinions and mindsets.

Every stronghold has a leader, a strongman. "When a strongman, fully armed, guards his own palace, his goods are in peace. But when a stronger than he comes upon him and overcomes him, he takes from him all his armor in which he trusted, and divides his spoils."⁶

We have to capture and bind the strongman,[7] before we can pull down the stronghold. But we have to know where to begin. "Works of the flesh," according to Galatians 5, are manifestations of spiritual strongmen.

> "Now the works of the flesh are evident, which are: adultery, fornication, uncleanness, lewdness, idolatry, sorcery, hatred, contentions, jealousies, outbursts of wrath, selfish ambitions, dissensions, heresies, envy, murders, [drunkenness, revelries, and the like; of which I tell you beforehand, just as I also told you in time past, that those who practice such things will not inherit the kingdom of God."[8]

Now let's look at a list of strongmen, where they are found in scripture and more examples of how they manifest.

LIST OF SPIRITUAL STRONGMEN

Spirit of Infirmity[9]

Examples: attacks on male and female identity, allergies, strange syndromes, bent body, asthma, cancer, arthritis.

Spirit of Fear[10]

Example: fright, torment, inferiority, inadequacy, worry, critical spirit, tension, nightmares, anxiety, untrusting, fears of anything.

Spirit of Pythos also known as Spirit of Divination[11]

Examples: rebellion, witchcraft, occult practices, black arts, magic, drugs, fortunetelling.

Spirit of Sexual Immorality also known as Spirit of Harlotry or Whoredom[12]

Examples: lust, adultery, pornography, rape, incest, (spirit, soul, or body) prostitution, love of money, chronic dissatisfaction, excessive appetite formation, worldliness.

Enslaving spirit: also known as Spirit of Bondage[13]

Examples: addictions, bulimia, anorexia, wrong relationships, codependency, fear of death, compulsive sin, bondage to sin.

Spirit of Pride: also known as Spirit of Haughtiness[14]

Example: Pride, scorn, mockery, lewdness, egotism, prejudice, arrogance, gossip, criticism, idleness, obstinate, self-deception, rejection of God, self-righteous.

Spirit of Perversion[15]

Examples: Homosexuality, sexual perversion, abnormal activism, broken spirit, evil actions, atheist, abortion, child abuse, filthy mind, doctrinal error, twisting the word, contentious, incest.

Spirit of Antichrist[16]

Examples: demons that take glory from Christ, denies the supernatural gifts, attributing them to Satan, opposes, harasses, persecute, Denies Deity of Christ, Humanism, teachers of heresies, deceiver, lawlessness.

Spirit of Depression or Heaviness[17]

Examples: depression, abnormal grief, despair, hopelessness, suicidal thoughts, insomnia, broken heart, self-pity, rejection, inner hurts, heaviness.

Lying Spirit[18]

Examples: unbelief, deception, compromise, flattery, legalism, superstitions, false prophecy accusations, slander, gossip, lies, false teachers.

Spirit of Jealousy[19]

Examples: jealousy, anger, rage, cruelty, suspicion, unnatural competition, divorce, revenge, spite, hatred envy, divisions.

Spirit of Stupor or Slumber[20]

Examples: constant fatigue, passivity, self-pity.

Dumb and Deaf Spirit[21]

Examples: Dumb(mute) crying, drowning, tearing, mental illness, blindness, ear problems, foaming at mouth, seizures/epilepsy, gnashing of teeth.

Familiar Spirit[22]

Examples: Necromancer, medium, clairvoyant, passive mind-dreamers, drugs, false prophecy.

Seducing Spirits[23]

Examples: hypocritical lies, seared conscience, attractions, fascinations, deception, wander from truth, fasciation to evil ways, seducers, enticers.

Spirit of Error[24]

Examples: error, unsubmissive, unteachable, servant of corruption, defensive/argumentative, new age.

I retrieved this information from different resources and condensed them into one comprehensive list. (See the references at the end of the book.)[25] This list shows the enemy's strongholds are all around us. We have become so comfortable with many of the manifestations of these spirits that we no longer see them as a problem. When people lie, we say they stretched the truth. When people have addictions, we say they are sick. When someone watches porn, we say all men do it. When we are jealous, we say there is something wrong with the other person. My point is that the general western cultures, including some churches, do not see or believe evil spirits are real. We see people with common, universal problems. We tend to either make excuses for the behavior or we judge them severely.

I have studied spiritual warfare for many years. I love to pray for people. As an intercessor, it is important to know God's word to know how to pray. Sometimes as I'm praying, I will see what to pray about, or I will hear a word or phrase in my spirit. This should be a very common experience for all Christians. We have been given the Holy Spirit and His gifts to teach us how to pray. These gifts began to develop in me as I studied scriptures. I purchased books, listened to podcast and sermons, and attended many conferences to learn more about what I was experiencing. The best teacher is the Holy Spirit.

I find as I get alone with God, He reveals hidden things, exposes the plans and strategies of the enemy, and gives me direction in how to pray. If you want God to speak to you in more ways than just in church on Sundays, you will need to find time to pray, stay, wait, and listen. Investing in resources that will teach and train you in these areas are highly recommended. The more familiar you are with a person, the easier the conversation. God is no different; the more you are familiar with Him the more you will understand how He speaks to you. Yes, God speaks to you!

I want to go a little deeper and share more about a few of the spirits in the list provided. Let me begin by sharing a vision I had from God, that brought great revelation knowledge and put my experience with evil spirits into perspective.

REJECTION

I saw a large black bat. It had its back turned to me. The creature had a stance like a man, even though I could identify it as a large bat. Its wings were folded in front because it was hiding something. When the bat turned around, its wings opened more and I could see pride, fear, rebellion, and many other things. I prayed and asked the Lord what this represented and the Lord said, "rejection."

To reject is "to refuse to have, take, recognize, to refuse to grant (a request, demand, etc.); to refuse to accept (someone or something); rebuff: to discard as useless or unsatisfactory: to cast out or eject; vomit. to cast out or off."[26] Rejection is the process or state of being rejected.

Rejection falls under the category of a spirit of depression or heaviness. It is something very common among the women I've mentored, but it is not exclusive to women. Men also experience rejection. I have found that men and women respond differently to it. We have all felt rejected at some point in our lives. I am no stranger to it at all. In fact, the vision of rejection propelled me to dig a little deeper into how destructive rejection can be. What I realized in that vision, is that rejection was hiding other problems. It was covering pride, fear, rebellion, jealousy, and so much more. Rejection is never alone and works with other spirits to destroy the fruit of the Holy Spirit living in us.

> "But the fruit of the Spirit is love, joy, peace, longsuffering, kindness, goodness, faithfulness, gentleness, self-control. Against such there is no law."[27]

> "Rejection is one of the most destructive spirits. It wreaks havoc on your life, preventing you from experiencing the fullness and blessings of God. It leads to destructive behaviors such as people-roaming, attention seeking, perfectionism, anger and bitterness, hard-heartedness, pride, isolation, addiction to drugs or alcohol, and sexual promiscuity. And after the spirit does its damage, rejection inevitably leaves lives desolated and in ruins."[28]

In fact, rejection produces the opposite of the fruit of the Holy Spirit, causing a ripple effect and opening the door to other strongmen. Rejection has to have an entrance point. Like all strongholds, there is a secret way in and out. In his book, *Destroying the Spirit of Rejection*, best-selling author John Eckhardt, lists several ways in which rejection can enter our lives. I highly recommend that every household have a copy of this book. It is informative and full of revelation knowledge that can be used to teach others or identity rejection in your own life. It is time we see where the enemy has been hiding in our families.

HOW DOES REJECTION ENTER?

- Rejection from the Womb
- Generational Rejection
- Stages of Life
- Parents' Relationships to Each Other

- Parents' Relationship to Their Children
- Sibling Dynamic
- Life-Changing Events or Trauma
- Involuntary Physical Characteristics
- School, Church, and Other Social Groups
- Rejection Later in Life

Self-rejection, fear of rejection, and the act of rejecting others form the core of the spirit of rejection. Rejection is a hurtful and painful experience that no one likes to go through. Many of us avoid it by almost any means necessary.[29]

Some Symptoms of Rejection
Addiction
Attention seeking
Despair
Discouragement
Envy
Fears
Frustration
Guilt
Loneliness
Pride
Revenge
Self-rejection
Shame
Suicide
Withdrawal"[30]

the process

Let's look at some biblical examples of rejection. The story of Jacob, Rachel and Leah is a good way to understand how rejection enters and how it wounds:

> "Now Laban had two daughters: the name of the elder was Leah, and the name of the younger was Rachel. Leah's eyes were delicate, but Rachel was beautiful of form and appearance."[31]

Right from the beginning, we see there was a distinct difference between the two daughters of Laban. "Leah's eyes were delicate." Leah was probably born with "delicate," eyes, which is also translated as "weak" eyes. She might have been treated differently because of her eyes and even teased by her sister, father, or others in her tribe. You can imagine the rejection Leah felt just because her eyes were weak. Next the scripture says, "but Rachel was beautiful of form and appearance." The two daughters were compared based on their physical differences. Comparison opens the door for rejection and jealousy. Leah was always trying to appear good enough due to her eyes, and Rachel was always given compliments for her beauty.

"Now Jacob loved Rachel; so he said, 'I will serve you seven years for Rachel your younger daughter.'"[32] Here Jacob is a single man now working for Laban to marry one of his daughters, Rachel, the "one he loved." Over the course of seven years, Jacob becomes part of the family, an extra hand for Laban and soon-to-be husband of Rachel. Jacob makes his desire known to Laban and commits to the deal. Read what Laban says:

> "And Laban said, 'It is better that I give her to you than that I should give her to another man. Stay with me.' So Jacob served seven years for Rachel, and they seemed only a few days to him because of the love he had for her.

> Then Jacob said to Laban, 'Give me my wife, for my days are fulfilled, that I may go in to her.' And Laban gathered together all the men of the place and made a feast. Now it came to pass in the evening, that he took Leah his daughter and brought her to Jacob; and he went in to her. And Laban gave his maid Zilpah to his daughter Leah as a maid. So it came to pass in the morning, that behold, it was Leah. And he said to Laban, "What is this you have done to me? Was it not for Rachel that I served you? Why then have you deceived me?"[33]

Laban gives Jacob the impression he was working for Rachel, the one he loved, but Laban has other plans. He prepares Leah, the eldest daughter, and deceives Jacob. Jacob enjoys the feast and sleeps with his bride, whom he believes is Rachel. You have to wonder what Leah is thinking about all this. She is aware Jacob loves Rachel and had asked for her hand in marriage, but she does not say a word. Perhaps Leah thinks Jacob will be fine once they are together. Maybe she thinks Jacob will, in turn, love her for her kindness. Granted, she does not have a choice; she is only obeying her father, and according to their tradition, she is to be married first. The next morning, Jacob realizes it was Leah he had married and is upset. He confronts Laban. Leah is crushed and rejected, yet again.

> "And Laban said, "It must not be done so in our country, to give the younger before the firstborn. Fulfill her week, and we will give you this one also for the service which you will serve with me still another seven years. Then Jacob did so and fulfilled her week. So he gave him his daughter Rachel as wife also. And Laban gave his maid Bilhah to his daughter Rachel as a maid. Then Jacob also went in to

> Rachel, and he also loved Rachel more than Leah. And he served with Laban still another seven years."[34]

Jacob serves another seven years for Rachel. "Then Jacob also went into Rachel, and he also loved Rachel more than Leah." Jacob stays to work for Rachel and she is given to him as his wife. Jacob is happy, and Rachel may be as well. But what about Leah? Does Leah experience rejection because of the family structure and traditions? Yes, she does, as well as her children. A few verses later, we see the Lord opening Leah's womb because she is unloved while Rachel is barren. Do you think Rachel feels rejected because she is barren? Remember the story about Hannah, who was barren and grieved and had "bitterness of soul?" Barrenness is a hard pill to swallow for many men and women who want to have natural children. Many times, the grief causes relationships to fail.

The practice of polygamy was common in biblical times. Certain cultures today still practice this type of family unit. Rivalry between co-wives and siblings was very common, and history has proven that this practice has many dysfunctions.

> "Instead of affording their wives the priceless blessings and opportunity to enjoy the uniqueness in marriage, women in polygamous marriages are forced to compete for their husband's affections, his attention and love for the rest of their lives. With the fear of becoming the loser, these women live in deep sense of insecurity. Polygamy actually stands in the way of the pledge binding husbands and wives. It also corrodes the natural alliance and sisterhood of women because they go to endlessly struggle for the same man."[35]

Rejection is a poison. Regardless of how it enters your life, it can affect you and your loved ones for many years. Jesus also experienced rejection. "He was despised and rejected by men, a man of sorrows, and acquainted with grief. And we esteemed him not."[36]

Jesus was perfect. There was no sin, no personality or character flaw in Him that caused Him to be rejected. He suffered undeserved rejection all His life, even though He healed the sick and delivered people from evil spirits. He was rejected by His disciples and peers, by His half-brothers, by His nation, by the Gentiles, and by the Jews. "He came to that which was His own, but His own did not receive Him. Yet to all who received Him, to those who believed in His name, He gave the right to become children of God."[37] He experienced the loneliness, suffering, and grief that comes along with rejection. "Surely He has borne our griefs and carried our sorrows, yet we esteemed Him stricken, smitten by God and afflicted."[38] Jesus even felt rejected by God, His Father. Remember His cry from the cross: "My God! My God! Why have you forsaken me?"[39] When Jesus became man, He bore the full penalty for our sin, which is separation from God: "By His wounds we are healed."[40]

> "For we do not have a high priest who is unable to sympathize with our weaknesses, but we have one who has been tempted in every way, just as we are—yet without sin. Let us then approach the throne of grace with confidence, so that we may receive mercy and find grace to help us in our time of need."[41]

SPIRIT OF FEAR

Manifestations of the spirit of fear include: fright, torment, fears of inferiority or inadequacy, worry, a critical spirit, tension, nightmares, anxiety, lack of trust, etc. The Bible mentions two kinds of fear. The "fear of the Lord" and the "spirit of fear." "The [reverent] fear of the Lord is the beginning (the prerequisite, the absolute essential, the alphabet) of wisdom."[42] The "fear of the Lord" is a position of deep respect and reverence we place ourselves in when we understand the nature of God. This kind of fear leads to wisdom, knowledge, and respect.

"For God did not give us a spirit of timidity or cowardice or fear, but [He has given us a spirit] of power and of love and of sound judgment and personal discipline [abilities that result in a calm, well-balanced mind and self-control]."[43] One the other hand, a spirit of fear destroys faith, joy, peace, and love. Notice the scripture says that instead of the spirit of fear, God gives us power (through the Holy Spirit) love (God is love) and a sound mind (discipline, stability, a well-balanced mind). There is no fear in love. Perfect love (God) casts out all fear.[44]

I never considered myself to by a fearful person. Sure, I was afraid of some things that are pretty common. I am fascinated by people and have a curiosity about them. I never meet a stranger, and I can talk to anyone. I'm not afraid of conflict or having a difficult conversation. I actually enjoy those types of conversations because I like to learn from different viewpoints. I am not the kind of person who is easily swayed by someone passionate about their view or choice.

I was in a Bible study and the topic for the week was fear. I turned to the pages of the assigned book, and I read that the author stated she had made decisions in her life based on fear. Immediately, I felt the Holy Spirit tell me to pause. I began to think about some of the decisions I have made, even recent decisions, and I was surprised to see how many were because I was in fear. I was afraid of something, but afraid of what? I didn't feel fearful because I thought someone would physically hurt me. I wasn't shy or afraid to talk to people. But there was a phobia. A phobia is "intense fear of certain situations, activities, things, animal or people," according to John Eckhardt.[45]

I had a fear of animals (especially dogs), wild animals (lions), car accidents, failing, and snakes. These fears were there even as a child. So, I dug a little deeper and made some discoveries.

I had been bitten by a dog as a child and became afraid of the mean dogs running around the neighborhood. I had nightmares about lions trying to eat me. We were in a car accident when I was a child. I could not eat pears for years because I was eating one at the time of the accident. Also, my brother was in a car accident, and I saw the bloody bandages wrapped around his head. As a musician, I had a fear that I would mess up a song. I still don't like snakes, but I had dreams in which I was killing them. These fears had been there all my life, but I did not see them as uncommon and unusual. I was used to them and thought that everyone was afraid of something.

I was having a conversation with my husband about the fears, and he told me he'd noticed other fears, such as a fear of flying, a fear of heights, and a fear of death. These were all fears that came on me as an adult. I never feared flying as a child. I grew up in Colorado and loved the mountains and activities such as hiking, skiing, etc. I wasn't afraid to die because I know Jesus.

Each of these fears must have a root cause for its existence in my life. So, I began to research why. I realized I was afraid to die, not because I thought I would go to hell, but because I did not want to leave my husband and I wanted to raise my children. I realized that doing anything that could cause me to die was out of the question, i.e. flying or falling from a great height. I have since been delivered from these kinds of fears because of prophetic words spoken over my life brought hope and crushed the spirit of fear.

In this same Bible study, one of the songs on our weekly playlist was, "No Longer Slaves" by Jonathan David and Melissa Helser with Bethel Music. The first time I heard the song, I cried for hours, playing it over and over again. I realized God was removing these fears that had keep me so bound. I encourage you to buy the song for your personal playlist. Here are some of the words; let this be your prayer.

> **No Longer Slaves**
> "You unravel me with a melody,
> You surround me with a song.
> Of deliverance from my enemies
> 'til all my fears are gone.
> I'm no longer a slave to fear
> I am a child of God…
>
> I am surrounded
> By the arms of the father.
> I am surrounded
> By songs of deliverance…
>
> We've been liberated
> From our bondage.
> We're the sons and the daughters
> Let us sing our freedom…
>
> You split the sea
> So I could walk right through it.
> My fears were drowned in perfect love.

You rescued me
And I will stand and sing
I am a child of God."[46]

SPIRIT OF PRIDE

The last spirit I want to talk about is the spirit of pride, also called the Leviathan spirit and the spirit of haughtiness. Manifestations include pride, scorn, mockery, lewdness, egotism, prejudice, arrogance, gossip, criticism, idleness, obstinate, self-deception, rejection of God, and self-righteousness. "Pride goes before destruction, and a haughty spirit before a fall. It is better to be humble in spirit with the lowly, than to divide the spoil with the proud (haughty, arrogant)."[47]

> "Within the rejection personality the spirit of pride convinces a person, "you really do have a lot to be proud of." This cluster of demons even helps "promote self-advertising publicity campaigns to convince others" and forces "the gauge of inferiorities and low self-image to rise to an unreasonable level, and covers over the warning of Proverbs 27:2 - 'Let another praise you, and not your own mouth; someone else, and not your own lips.'"[48]

MY EXPERIENCE WITH LEVIATHAN

In the summer of 2016, I was praying about a difficult relationship. I also knew this person had a hard time hearing and often could not follow instructions due to a lack of understanding. However, it was more than that. I noticed a pattern of miscommunication and misinterpretation of our conversations, and I felt as if this individual was not clearly hearing what was being said. Did I just describe someone you know?

I began to pray about this relationship, because every time they were around, I could feel a battle before it even started. This persisted for several months, and finally I'd had enough. I prayed right before I went to bed a simple prayer, "Lord, what is it I'm discerning?" This is a common prayer I prayed as an intercessor. I fell asleep and woke up late the next morning. I grabbed my phone to check the time, and I noticed an email notification from *XP Ministries* titled, "*Global Demonic Assault Revealed.*" I opened the email and read the description that was above the video. "Leviathan Exposed," was in bold letters, and it read:

> "Have you been struggling with relationship challenges? Has your business, ministry, or calling been under assault? Does it feel like there are swirls, confusion, miscommunication, and misunderstanding every time you turn around? Well, it is not by chance, and it certainly isn't just your imagination. There is a global assault by a high-level demonic spirit against the Body of Christ. On this week's episode of Everlasting Love TV, author and minister Robert Hotchkin joins Patricia King to discuss what is happening in the spirit and share keys to how you can overcome this assault and live in the victory and freedom Christ has given you."[49]

I said, "God, that was fast." I knew immediately this was going to give me answers as to why this relationship was so difficult. Robert and Patricia talked, and I was glued to my computer the whole 28 minutes and 30 seconds. This teaching was so eye-opening on so many levels that I ordered several copies of the book, *"Leviathan Exposed, Overcoming the Hidden Schemes of a Demonic King"* by Robert Hotchkin. Although I have read many other books and articles about Leviathan, I'm going to use his book to share a couple of points.

In chapter 2, "The Spirit of Leviathan," Hotchkin uses Isaiah 27:1 to describe Leviathan:

> A Fleeing Serpent:
>
> "I believe the Hebrew word baruch that is translated into English here as "fleeing" has more to do with the side-to-side, darting movement of the serpent, as opposed to the concept of retreating. The NIV translates bariach as "gliding." The NLT as "swiftly moving." The KJV and NKJV as "piercing." It appears that what the Lord is showing us here is that Leviathan darts from side to side in a conversation (whether it be verbal, emails, texts, etc.) to create misunderstanding and misinterpretation on both parts, causing one side to lash out at the other in an escalating war of offensive, accusations, hurt feelings, and embittered reactions."[50]

Notice Hotchkin said, "on both parts." This means that both parties in a conversation are victims of this spirit. I recognized I was frustrated and reacted to everything they had to say, good or bad.

> A Twisted Serpent:
>
> "The Hebrew word used for 'serpent' here is nachash. It means 'a snake (from its hiss)' and is derived from the root word meaning 'to whisper a spell.'
>
> Leviathan whispers wrong interpretations of what is being communicated to trigger offense and 'torture people with hurt feelings, bitterness, and resentment as to stir up anger, arguments, and overreactions.'"[51]

I remember having a vision of a snake whispering in the ears of a person I was praying for. At the time, I did not know it was a Leviathan spirit. I was aware the communication in their relationship was bad and I got the sense there was division. Leviathan tries to divide and conquer.

A Dragon that Lives in the Seas:

"And Leviathan plays a part in that it works to twist our thinking, understanding, and decisions so that we make wrong choices but feel justified in them. The word 'dragon' in Isaiah 27:1 is that Hebrew tannin from the root tan which means 'to elongate.' When something is elongated, it is stretched to the point of being misshapen. That is exactly what this spirit does in communication it takes what a person says and misshapes it so what is heard is not what was meant."[52]

This was exactly what I was experiencing. Even the simplest directions or updates given were "misshaped." I would often leave the conversation with the thought, "How did that get so screwed up?"

King Over the Sons of Pride:

"This is what Job 41:34 says about Leviathan: Leviathan is a king; not just some low-level demon or spirit, but a major principality. The other thing we discover is that this spirit rules and reigns over people who are "of pride." Every king has a domain (the word "kingdom," the place where a king has rule, is a shortened compound of "king's domain"). We give place to Leviathan, and invite it to rule and reign, when we enter into pride."[53]

Pride brings us into alignment with Leviathan. Pride will open the door for relationships to be under attack. Robert uses the word "principality" to describe the spirit. Job 41 talks about how fierce Leviathan can be. After hearing Job complain and blame God for all he was going through, God says to Job in Job 40:2-5:

> "Will the one who contends with the Almighty correct him? Let him who accuses God answer him!"[54]

God wanted Job to see that He was God alone. He corrected Job and showed him his own pride. Job's answer to God was full of humility. Humility is what breaks the grasp of Leviathan and releases the ungodly alignment.

> "Then Job answered the Lord: 'I am unworthy—how can I reply to you? I put my hand over my mouth. I spoke once, but I have no answer—twice, but I will say no more.'"[55]

How many time have you had to put your hands over your mouth? I have had to many times. Sometimes we think we know everything God is doing and that we have the right to correct Him when we don't agree with His methods. God confronted Job again, this time showing him how powerful Leviathan was and that only He could tame it:

> "Can you draw out Leviathan with a fishhook?
> Or press down his tongue with a cord?
> Can you put a rope [made] of rushes into his nose
> Or pierce his jaw through with a hook?
> Will he make many supplications to you [begging to be spared]?
> Or will he speak soft words to you [to coax you to treat him kindly]?

Will he make a covenant or an arrangement with you?
Will you take him for your servant forever?
Will you play with him as with a bird?
Or will you bind him [and put him on a leash] for your maidens?
Will traders bargain over him?
Will they divide him up among the merchants?
Can you fill his skin with harpoons,
Or his head with fishing spears?
Lay your hand on him;
Remember the battle [with him]; you will not do such [an ill-advised thing] again!
Behold, his [assailant's] hope and expectation [of defeating Leviathan] is false;
Will not one be overwhelmed even at the sight of him?
No one is so fierce [and foolhardy] that he dares to stir up Leviathan;
Who then is he who can stand before Me [or dares to contend with Me, the beast's creator]?"[56]

That is a powerful beast, but God is greater. "Lay your hand on him; remember the battle [with him]; you will not do such [an ill-advised thing] again!" I remember going to my prayer closet and praying against this spirit. I was determined that I was not going to be a victim of twisted mishap conversations anymore. These conversations were exhausting and I become increasingly irritated every time I was around them. I prayed and prayed and suffered five days with a headache—not because I did not have the power and authority through Jesus' name but because I had something in common with Leviathan: pride. I needed to repent and I did.

So, I will ask you, what do you have in common with Leviathan?

Pride puts us in alignment with him regardless of who we are. I think all of us are prideful to some degree. We all have things we like to brag about, our accomplishments, gifts, the way God is using us in ministry, income, etc. We also do not like to be wrong about our personal convictions and the issues we feel strongly about. When we are wounded, pride is often the first line of defense to protect ourselves from further injury. But clearly, humility is a better way. As I continued to pray and repent in humility, God said to me the key is to stay "low," prostrate, ground level, and not too high. As the Scriptures say, 'God opposes the proud but favors the humble' humble yourselves before God. Resist the devil, and he will flee from you."[57]

Do you want God to oppose you or give you favor? Who in their right mind would want God, the Almighty, to oppose them? I want God's grace and favor on my life every day. "Job said to the Lord, 'I had only heard about you before, but now I have seen you with my own eyes. I take back everything I said, and I sit in dust and ashes to show my repentance.'"[58] God is powerful, just and righteous. We love those attributes when they work in our favor, but when we feel an injustice because of our painful circumstances, we raise our fist to God. Job realized he was not only prideful but he did not know the ways of God.

So Job repented, and we need to repent as well. It is only through repentance, humility, and the Holy Spirit that we can defeat this king. "Now repent of your sins and turn to God, so that your sins may be wiped away. The times of refreshment will come from the presence of the Lord, and He will again send you Jesus, your appointed Messiah."[59]

ACTIVATION

Read and write Psalm 27.

ACTIVATION PRAYER

Most holy and powerful God, I have sinned against You because I have put myself in alignment with Leviathan through pride. I repent. I have been wounded by what I believed to be unfair situations that came into my life and out of my wounds I questioned Your character and tried to correct You, because I did not understand fully who You are. I do know You love me with an everlasting love and nothing can separate me from that love. Forgive me for the times when I was prideful about my accomplishments, gifts, income, status, etc. It is only through You that I am who I am today. In Jesus' name, Amen.

CHAPTER 9
victim or victor

WHAT IS A VICTIM?

> "A victim is a person harmed, injured, or killed as a result of a crime, accident, or other event or action."[1]

I remember that day like it was yesterday. I got up early and put on my navy-blue skirt suit with navy pantyhose and navy three-inch heels. I looked in the mirror but still wasn't ready to go downstairs, so I decided to add some pearls. My mom called from the kitchen, "Audra, are you going to eat?" "No, I'm not hungry. Let's just go." I walked downstairs but refused to look my mom in the eyes for fear I would see disappointment. We got in the car and drove downtown to the courthouse to file papers for a restraining order against my boyfriend at the time. As I saw the taunting courthouse building to my right, fear gripped my throat. But then my mom said, "Here it is, this is the address," and she pointed to a beautiful craftsman-style house that had been there for many decades.

The law office, once a home, made a timely statement that said, "Welcome home." I began to walk up the stairs leading to the massive, perfectly crafted wood door. My heart sank because I was not coming to this house to be welcomed by the lady of the house. No, I had to come face to face with the memories of a painful night. I opened the door and was greeted by the law office secretary, who smiled as she looked me over.

"Are you here to file a restraining order?" I just looked and nodded my head. She ushered my mother to the waiting room and said to me, "Follow me." As we walked to the next room, I could hear the creaking of the old wood floor, making my entrance known. I was handed a thick packet and was led into the grand dining room. Only there was no food in dainty dishes—it was a place to confront horrible memories of the past, some as recent as the night before. At the stained wooden oval table sat several women in silence, never looking to see who just walked into the room or at each other.

No one smiled at me; no one acknowledged my presence. The room was silent, still, and cold. Even with a spectacular chandelier that dropped perfectly in the center of the room, there was no awe, no joy, no glory. As I looked around the room, I could see casts wrapped around arms, bloodstained lips, disfigured noses, black eyes, and stitches holding together deep gashes. I sat silently in horror and dropped my face to the packet, fighting back tears that blurred my vision. Then I began to write.

Anxiety rose up in me. Conflicting voices shouted in my head, telling me to get out of there. I didn't belong there. I deserved to look like them. But then the familiar small voice spoke calmly words of encouragement and love. I almost forgot how to respond to this voice because for so long I'd ignored its warning about this relationship. How could I be sitting in the midst of abuse, terror, and fear but still hear encouragement and love guiding me through the sea of pages, reminding me of one of the darkest nights of my life? Why did I feel comfort but not see it in the room? Why was I wound-free and scar-free? How did I make it out of that moment without a scratch or scrape? There might not have been any physical evidence on my body, but the emotional and spiritual effects of that night were just as real.

Although I was a victim of abuse by a former boyfriend, I did not see myself as a victim. I refused to see myself as a victim, and my personal promise was not to tell anyone about it, ever again. I wanted to forget about it and move on, but my parents knew better. They had more insight into my personal situation then I did. They knew if I did not end it with a bold statement and firm action, I would not be safe. I would put myself back into a place of danger. Reluctantly, I followed through with their wise advice, and several court dates later, saga ended. I sent a clear message to my abuser that his actions were unacceptable. He never contacted me again, but God later gave him an opportunity to apologize.

LIFE GOES ON

The process that summer was humiliating. Not only were my parents and I fearful for my safety, but I felt as if I brought shame on them. I was not to blame for his actions, but I did ignore sound advice and remained in an unstable relationship. This led to an unnecessary roller coaster of emotions, arguments, breakups, control, and soon after, stalking and abuse.

the process

A year later, I graduated from college, and I wanted to work part-time for a season before going to finish my teaching certification. I got a job working in a department store selling cosmetics. With college behind me and a bright future in education ahead of me, I felt a great sense of accomplishment and achievement. I developed a relationship with several of the ladies in the department and had a chance hear about their lives. On slow nights, we would group together and share our latest stories. Most of the time, the stories were about their husbands, boyfriends, kids and grandkids alike. But the most heart-wrenching conversations were about their current painful relationships, whether husband or boyfriend. Some gloated and held their heads high, while others cried. I just kept silent.

While working one evening, I remember seeing a man ducking behind the clothing racks. His head bobbed up and down as he tried to conceal himself. Two security men from the store were hanging around the fragrance counter pretending to make a purchase. Next thing I knew, they whispered to the employee who worked in the counter next to mine and rushed her out. She came back the next day, upset and very tearful. I asked her if there was anything I could do to help her, which unleashed a river of tears. She began to tell me about the man who was ducking behind the clothing rack. He was an ex-boyfriend who had assaulted her on many occasions and was currently stalking her. She had a restraining order, but he ignored every warning. Here was my opportunity to share with her and let her know I understood, but I kept silent.

The department hired two new employees. They were working a cosmetic counter by themselves and had no one to really train them because we were without a manager at the time. They were both younger than I was and needed to learn the ropes. I began to train them, and we started hanging out periodically after work. As we began to share more about ourselves, one of the girls asked me if I knew a certain man who had attended the same high school I did. I said, of course I did, he was a former classmate. She talked about how in love they were and said they were going to get married. I was so excited and asked what he was up to. She told me he was in prison. I will call her Tammy. The other young lady I trained was living with her boyfriend; I will call her Beth. She spoke highly of him, but I knew something wasn't right.

At the beginning of the shift, I saw Beth cleaning the glass counter case. Her head was down, and she didn't speak. When I approached her, she looked up—she had a busted lip, a swollen black eye, and she was completely emotionally empty. I asked her what had happened, and she just said her boyfriend's name. I didn't push her, but I prayed silently. The security team had been alerted about the incident and were watching on the floor that day. No sooner then she had started her shift, she was quickly taken away when her angry boyfriend was spotted in the store. Months passed, and both Tammy and Beth seemed like normal young working women, but I was burdened to pray for them every time I saw them. Beth never said another word about the assault, and neither did I. I kept silent.

TIME TO SHARE

Chili's restaurant was across the street thus a frequent hang-out for us. The conversation started out the same, but this time I heard that still small voice urging me to speak about my incident, almost a year earlier to the date. I reluctantly shared my story, and both Tammy and Beth began to cry. Tammy shared that she was afraid to leave her boyfriend because he was very controlling and abusive. I wondered to myself, "How was it he could still keep her living in fear while he was in prison?" She explained he would control her through his mom and other friends.

This made me so mad, and I began to speak against the fear and control. They cried, and cried out for help. The only help I knew to give them was Jesus. So, I asked if they knew Jesus as savior and told them He could help them have the courage to leave these poisonous relationships. I lead them in the sinner's prayer. Tammy repented, and Beth rededicated her life to the Lord. I was no longer silent, because at that point I knew God was divinely aligning these relationships to bring them into a greater understanding and revelation knowledge of Jesus.

Tammy began coming to Wednesday night Bible study with me and continued her walk with the Lord. Beth continued her relationship with the same abusive boyfriend. I don't know where they are today, but God does. It was the season for me to open my mouth about my abuse and show others the healing power of God through Jesus. Through my obedience to share that experience, God took care of me and brought vindication when I least expected it.

APOLOGIES DON'T ALWAYS COME IN WORDS

My counter was next to the fragrance department. One slow evening, I turned around to see my ex-boyfriend buying women's perfume. I was frozen and speechless because I never expected to see him again. He turned around and was just as frozen and speechless as I was. Then with a soft voice he said, "Hi, how are you?" His face was sad. The excitement of buying a gift disappeared, and he just stood there looking at me. I waved, and he turned around, walked down the aisle, and went out the door. A river of emotions flooded my heart, and the tears began to run down my face. No matter what I tried to do, I could not stop crying. He did not apologize with his words, but I knew in his heart he was sorry. I never heard or saw him again. But I had truly forgiven him.

MINDSET OF A VICTIM

Earlier, I said I wanted to leave the abuse behind me. I did not see myself as a victim. To be honest, it was pride that kept my mouth shut. After all, how could this have happened to me? I was a preacher's kid, well-loved and well-educated. I had just finished my degree and was set to become a teacher. There was nothing holding me back.

That incident opened my eyes to some truth about myself. One, I had been disobedient to my father about his warning. My father is a praying man and never had peace about my dating this guy. I thought I was grown and could discern for myself, so I ignored his fatherly warning. In my mind, my dad wasn't going to like anyone I dated; he never had before, and I was used to his disapproval. I honestly thought he would get over it. I wanted so much for him to approve. At that point, I decided I wasn't going to date anyone unless my father was aware and gave his blessing. I knew my dad would identify who my future husband was, and he did.

The next thing I learned was that I was prideful. I was too proud to tell my story of an abusive situation. Going thought it was humiliating enough—why would I share that humiliation with someone else? I was more concerned with my reputation than the pain and fear that many women face each day from their abusers. Once I broke my silence, the door was open for me to talk about Jesus. God began the healing process within me so I could forgive, and he also developed in me a compassion for women.

I said I was not a victim, even though by definition, I was. But I did not have a victim mentality. This meant I took full responsibility for my actions and my part of the relationship. I did not blame him or even try to demonize him. I was fully aware this was not a good relationship for either of us. I was warned by several people, not just my parents. Thank God for the godly women who could see the danger I was in and spoke up. Thank God for my friend and future husband, who also warned me.

The true victim mentality, according to Wikipedia, "is an acquired personality trait in which a person tends to recognize themselves as a victim of the negative actions of others, and to behave as if this were the case in the face of clear evidence of such circumstances."[2] Here are a few other important characteristics of a person with a victim mentality:

- "People who are victims usually don't see that the only thing in common between all the people and situations they think they have been victimized by is themselves.
- Victims usually are people you can't depend on, because they deny responsibility for their actions. They are quick to blame other people and situations for anything that doesn't work in their lives.
- Victims don't have resilience, which is the ability to quickly bounce back after being knocked down.
- Victims generally are passive.
- Victims are usually angry at the people or events they think have "done them wrong," and underneath the feeling of anger is almost always the feeling of powerlessness.
- Successful people are rarely victims. One might be able to be a victim and still make money and have great

relationships in rare cases, but usually it would be difficult for victims to be successful. To be successful you need to learn from your mistakes and try again. Victims are, by definition, people who do not acknowledge responsibility for their actions and who blame outside forces."[3]

This type of mentality produces behaviors that trap people. It does not allow them to move forward and beyond their current situation. It prevents them from being productive and stifles their desire to improve, advance, and dream. It knocks the breath of life right out of them and causes them to be stagnant, all the while blaming other people for their lack of movement. It causes them to not be accountable for their own actions.

Although I was victimized, I fought to redefine what that meant. I finished my degree the following year, worked for a time, and then began a new career working as an esthetician and professional makeup artist at a local spa. This gave me the opportunity to speak into the lives of many women every day. I had big dreams to develop my own skincare and makeup line. That incident was not going to define me. I knew at that time, I had the power to help women who were once victims to be victorious.

TRUTH SETS US FREE

In 1996, I had my twenty-fifth birthday. My friends, family, and I celebrated this momentous occasion. The next day was Monday, and the spa I worked at was closed. I sat in my room, opened my Bible, and began to let the Holy Spirit speak to me. He began to show me faces of girls I had known in the past. They all had something in common, I hated them for various reasons.

The Holy Spirit whispered, "You need to forgive her; I want you to forgive her; you need to forgive her, now. Let her go—don't hold her in your heart anymore. Forgive." I was overwhelmed with His presence and began to speak out loud, "Lord, I forgive her; I forgive them. Please help me to truly forgive."

This happened for three consecutive days. Tears of freedom and peace filled my room. A weight had been lifted off my shoulders that I did not realized I was carrying. I felt lighter, brighter, happier, and I could see the light of love God had for these girls and women who had hurt me. Yes, He loved them just like He loved me. He was always aware of how they'd treated me, and He was aware of how I treated them. Yet His love covered me like a soft blanket, and I was consumed with His peace.

"Hate" was a word I often used to describe how I felt about women. I would say things like, "I hate girls, I don't like girls, I don't want to hang with girls, I get along better with guys." I had no compassion for women, no love. Why? Here is my list:

    Girls are bullies.
    Girls don't like me.
    Girls turn others against me.
    Girls are jealous.
    Girls steal boyfriends.
    Girls always compare themselves to others.
    Girls have something negative to say about other girls.
    Girls cheat and lie.
    The only girls I will hang out with are girls who hate other girls.

You are laughing and smiling, I know. It is because you can relate to my list of offenses against girls. But isn't it sad? The very things I hated are the very things I did. I was guilty of all of them. Paul says, "I have discovered this principle of life—that when I want to do what is right, I inevitably do what is wrong."[4] When God began to show me the truth about why I felt justified in hating women, I could not believe He was showing me myself. "Then you will know the truth, and the truth will set you free."[5] Knowing the truth about why you feel the way you do releases the freedom to change.

For such a long time, I had seen myself as a victim in almost every relationship with girls. I had a negative attitude towards women because I believed all my issues stemmed from my relationships with them. I had begun to develop a victim mentality every time there was a new conflict with a female.

> "And the Holy Spirit helps us in our weakness. For example, we don't know what God wants us to pray for. But the Holy Spirit prays for us with groanings that cannot be expressed in words. And the Father who knows all hearts knows what the Spirit is saying, for the Spirit pleads for us believers in harmony with God's own will. And we know that God causes everything to work together for the good of those who love God and are called according to his purpose for them."[6]

With this victim mentality, I was always blaming women for my problems. I did not know how to pray for them and really did not want to. It was the Holy Spirit who spoke truth to me and set me free to begin to pray for them. He gave me the words. He showed me the hurt. The very area of my life that had been the most painful for many years, was the very place where God showed me my purpose and called me to work for Him. He worked everything out. My hatred and mistrust of women, and my lack of compassion for them soon turned into a deep love and concern. He turned my pain into purpose. He called me to equip and activate women into their purpose by teaching them their true identity and mentoring them in developing beautiful character. If this was my purpose and assignment then I needed to have the love for them that He did. This turned out to be a very long process. God wants us to be victorious in all we do and He wanted me to show women how they could be victorious in Him. Victorious means "having achieved a victory; conquering; triumphant."[7]

Joseph Mattera, wrote in "Daily Blog: Emotional Health." In his article, he gave several contrasts between a victim and victorious mindset. Here are some examples Joseph gave. I would encourage you to read the through the list and ask God to show you where there is need to change your mindset from victim to victor.

1. The victim sees a challenge as an obstacle.
   The victor sees the obstacle as an opportunity.
2. The victim depends on handouts from others to succeed.
   The victor makes do with what they already have to succeed.
3. The victim only sees closed doors.
   The victor only sees open doors.
4. The victim spreads a negative attitude to others.
   The victor spreads a positive attitude.
5. The victim is pessimistic.
   The victor is optimistic.
6. The victim gives up quickly if they don't succeed.

The victor doesn't quit until they succeed.

7. The victim repels people.
   The victor attracts people.

8. The victim is always fighting for "my rights."
   The victor lives to champion the rights of others.

9. The victim has a critical spirit and is judgmental of others.
   The victor blesses others.

10. The victim imagines people are against them.
    The victor imagines people are for them.

11. The victim plays on the emotions of others.
    The victor releases the passion of others.

12. The victim uses people for what they can get.
    The victor is a catalyst to inspire people to flourish.[8]

ACTIVATION

Are you a victim or a victor? God wants you to be a victor. Do a Bible search for the scriptures that support the victory we have in Christ. Write them down and begin to pray them over yourself.

ACTIVATION PRAYER

Today Lord, I am thankful because I have victory in You. I don't have to live with a victim mentality. I choose to be a person who sees open doors, has a positive attitude, attracts the right people, blesses others and releases compassion for others. I release anyone from my heart who had made me feel less than. In Jesus' name, Amen.

CHAPTER 10
God's process for salvation

This is the most important part of the process. For some of you, this book may be your first introduction to God. For others, it may be a clearer view of how He works things out on your behalf. He wants you to be free. You have learned that God's view of you is in relation to who He is and have learned some of His amazing attributes. You have read about Jesus, heard of His compassion, and prayed in His name in the Activation Prayers. For some, you have received Jesus as your savior, accepted His sacrifice for your sins but you never knew the Holy Spirit. This chapter will answer some of the questions you might have about the only true God. He is the one who created the universe. He is also the one who created you in His image, heals your wounds, resolves your issues, defeats every enemy and purposes you for victory.

God has a process for salvation. I grew up in a Baptist church, and every Sunday we recited the "Confession of Faith." It was printed in our weekly bulletin for the whole congregation to read in unison. I cannot remember when I first learned it, but it was so embedded in my head that I recited every word from memory. In the order of service, someone different each Sunday, was assigned to lead the church in this great statement of faith, and with one voice we would say:

CONFESSION OF FAITH—ZION BAPTIST CHURCH

> "I believe in God, the Father Almighty,
> the Creator of heaven and earth,
> and in Jesus Christ, his only Son, our Lord;
> Who was conceived by the Holy Spirit,
> born of the Virgin Mary,
> suffered under Pontius Pilate,
> was crucified, died, and was buried.
> The third day he arose again from the dead.
> He ascended into heaven
> and sits at the right hand of God the Father Almighty,
> whence he shall come to judge the living and the dead.
> I believe in the Holy Spirit,
> the holy universal Church,
> the communion of saints,
> the forgiveness of sins,
> the resurrection of the body,
> and the life everlasting. Amen"[1]

I later found out that our church's Confession of Faith was also called the Apostles' Creed. This confession or creed is a comprehensive, scripture-supported, powerful statement that should become a foundation for every Christian. It is a summary of the vital points of faith in a believer's life. Through research, I discovered that there are many versions of the creed, adapted by other evangelical denominations as well as the Catholic church. The version above was adapted for the Baptist church I grew up in.

I believe the creed is a great example of God's process for salvation. The Apostles' Creed has eighteen essential and fundamental points to explore, I included scripture to support each statement.

18 ESSENTIAL POINTS

1. Believe in God

    "But without faith it is impossible to [walk with God and] please Him, for whoever comes [near] to God must [necessarily] believe that God exists and that He rewards those who [earnestly and diligently] seek Him."[2]

2. God as the Father Almighty

    "And, 'I will be a Father to you, and you will be my sons and daughters, says the Lord Almighty.'"[3]

3. God as the Creator

    "In the beginning God (Elohim) created [by forming from nothing] the heavens and the earth. The earth was formless and void or a waste and emptiness, and darkness was upon the face of the deep [primeval ocean that covered the unformed earth]."[4]

4. Jesus Christ was introduced as God's only son

    "For God, so [greatly] loved and dearly prized the world, that He [even] gave His [One and] only begotten Son, so that whoever believes and trusts in Him [as Savior] shall not perish, but have eternal life."[5]

5. Jesus Christ as Lord

"He [Christ] is the image of the invisible God, the firstborn over all creation."[6]

"Therefore God also has highly exalted Him and given Him the name which is above every name,[10] that at the name of Jesus every knee should bow, of those in heaven, and of those on earth, and of those under the earth,[11] and that every tongue should confess that Jesus Christ is Lord, to the glory of God the Father."[7]

6. Jesus' miraculous conception by the Holy Spirit and born of the virgin Mary

"Now the birth of Jesus Christ was as follows: when His mother Mary had been betrothed to Joseph, before they came together she was found to be with child by [the power of] the Holy Spirit. And Joseph her [promised] husband, being a just and righteous man and not wanting to expose her publicly to shame, planned to send her away and divorce her quietly.

But after he had considered this, an angel of the Lord appeared to him in a dream, saying, 'Joseph, descendant of David, do not be afraid to take Mary as your wife, for the Child who has been conceived in her is of the Holy Spirit. She will give birth to a Son, and you shall name Him Jesus (The Lord is salvation), for He will save His people from their sins.' All this happened in order to fulfill what the Lord had spoken through the prophet [Isaiah]: 'Behold, the virgin shall be with child and give birth to a Son, and they shall call His name Immanuel'—which, when translated, means, 'God with us.'

Then Joseph awoke from his sleep and did as the angel of the Lord had commanded him, and he took Mary [to his home] as his wife, but he kept her a virgin until she had given birth to a Son [her firstborn child]; and he named Him Jesus (The Lord is salvation)."[8]

7. Under the governmental leader, Pontius Pilate

"When Pilate heard this, he brought Jesus out and sat down on the judge's seated a place known as the Stone Pavement (which in Aramaic is Gabbatha). It was the day of Preparation of the Passover; it was about noon."
'Here is your king,' Pilate said to the Jews.
But they shouted, 'Take him away! Take him away! Crucify him!'
'Shall I crucify your king?' Pilate asked.
'We have no king but Caesar,' the chief priests answered.
Finally Pilate handed him over to them to be crucified."[9]

8. Jesus died on the cross

"And when Jesus had cried out again in a loud voice, he gave up his spirit."[10]

"Jesus called out with a loud voice, 'Father, into your hands I commit my spirit.' When he had said this, he breathed his last."[11]

"Later, knowing that everything had now been finished, and so that Scripture would be fulfilled, Jesus said, 'I am thirsty.' A jar of wine vinegar was there, so they soaked a sponge in it, put the sponge on a stalk of the hyssop plant, and lifted it to Jesus' lips. When he had received the drink, Jesus said, 'It is finished.' With that, he bowed his head and gave up his spirit."[12]

9. Jesus was buried in a grave on earth

"As evening approached, there came a rich man from Arimathea, named Joseph, who had himself become a disciple of Jesus. Going to Pilate, he asked for Jesus' body, and Pilate ordered that it be given to him. Joseph took the body, wrapped it in a clean linen cloth, and placed it in his own new tomb that he had cut out of the rock. He rolled a big stone in front of the entrance to the tomb and went away."[13]

"Joseph of Arimathea, a prominent member of the Council, who was himself waiting for the kingdom of God, went boldly to Pilate and asked for Jesus' body. Pilate was surprised to hear that he was already dead. Summoning the centurion, he asked him if Jesus had already died. When he learned from the centurion that it was so, he gave the body to Joseph. So Joseph bought some linen cloth, took down the body, wrapped it in the linen, and placed it in a tomb cut out of rock. Then he rolled a stone against the entrance of the tomb."[14]

"Going to Pilate, he asked for Jesus' body. Then he took it down, wrapped it in linen cloth and placed it in a tomb cut

God's salvation process

in the rock, one in which no one had yet been laid."[15]

"Taking Jesus' body, the two of them wrapped it, with the spices, in strips of linen. This was in accordance with Jewish burial customs. At the place where Jesus was crucified, there was a garden, and in the garden a new tomb, in which no one had ever been laid. Because it was the Jewish day of Preparation and since the tomb was nearby, they laid Jesus there."[16]

10. Jesus' resurrection from the dead

"After the Sabbath, at dawn on the first day of the week, Mary Magdalene and the other Mary went to look at the tomb. There was a violent earthquake, for an angel of the Lord came down from heaven and, going to the tomb, rolled back the stone and sat on it. His appearance was like lightning, and his clothes were white as snow. he guards were so afraid of him that they shook and became like dead men. The angel said to the women, 'Do not be afraid, for I know that you are looking for Jesus, who was crucified. He is not here; he has risen, just as he said. Come and see the place where he lay.'"[17]

"When the Sabbath was over, Mary Magdalene, Mary the mother of James, and Salome bought spices so that they might go to anoint Jesus' body. Very early on the first day of the week, just after sunrise, they were on their way to the tomb and they asked each other, "Who will roll the stone away from the entrance of the tomb?" But when they looked up, they saw that the stone, which was very large, had been rolled away. As they entered the tomb, they saw a young man dressed in a white robe sitting on the right side, and they were alarmed. "Don't be alarmed," he said. "You are looking for Jesus the Nazarene, who was crucified. He has risen! He is not here. See the place where they laid him."[18]

11. Jesus' ascension; Jesus is now seated in heaven

"After the Lord Jesus had spoken to them, he was taken up into heaven and he sat at the right hand of God."[19]

"When he had led them out to the vicinity of Bethany, he lifted up his hands and blessed them. While he was blessing them, he left them and was taken up into heaven."[20]

"Then they gathered around him and asked him, "Lord, are you at this time going to restore the kingdom to Israel?" He said to them: "It is not for you to know the times or dates the Father has set by his own authority. But you will receive power when the Holy Spirit comes on you; and you will be my witnesses in Jerusalem, and in all Judea and Samaria, and to the ends of the earth." After he said this, he was taken up before their very eyes, and a cloud hid him from their sight. They were looking intently up into the sky as he was going, when suddenly two men dressed in white stood beside them. 'Men of Galilee,' they said, 'why do you stand here looking into the sky? This same Jesus, who has been taken from you into heaven, will come back in the same way you have seen him go into heaven.'"[21]

"The power is the same as the mighty strength he exerted when he raised Christ from the dead and seated him at his right hand in the heavenly realms, far above all rule and authority, power and dominion, and every name that is invoked, not only in the present age but also in the one to come."[22]

12. Jesus will judge the quick (living) and the dead

"In the presence of God and of Christ Jesus, who will judge the living and the dead, and in view of his appearing and his kingdom, I give you this charge."[23]

13. Introduction of the Holy Spirit which completed the Trinity of God

"Therefore go and make disciples of all nations, baptizing them in the name of the Father and of the Son and of the Holy Spirit."[24]

"Do not leave Jerusalem, but wait for the gift my Father promised, which you have heard me speak about. For John baptized with[a] water, but in a few days you will be baptized with the Holy Spirit."[25]

"But the fruit of the Spirit [the result of His presence within us] is love [unselfish concern for others], joy, [inner] peace, patience [not the ability to wait, but how we act while waiting], kindness, goodness, faithfulness, gentleness, self-control. Against such things there is no law."[26]

14. The Holy Universal Church

"Notice the church, Jesus Christ is the foundation of the church and the chief corner stone. The church is also the Bride of Christ. "Saints" in the New Testament refers to baptized believers in a local congregation, such as the saints at Corinth, or Ephesus, or Colossae. Some of these believers were far from saintly in their behavior, but they were holy by virtue of their participation (communio) in Christ."[27]

15. The Communion of Saints

"So I, the prisoner for the Lord, appeal to you to live a life worthy of the calling to which you have been called [that is, to live a life that exhibits godly character, moral courage, personal integrity, and mature behavior—a life that expresses gratitude to God for your salvation], with all humility [forsaking self-righteousness], and gentleness [maintaining self-control], with patience, bearing with one another in [unselfish] love. Make every effort to keep the oneness of the Spirit in the bond of peace [each individual working together to make the whole successful]. There is one body [of believers] and one Spirit—just as you were called to one hope when called [to salvation]—one Lord, one faith, one baptism, one God and Father of us all who is [sovereign] over all and [working] through all and [living] in all."[28]

16. The Forgiveness of Sins

"If we [freely] admit that we have sinned and confess our sins, He is faithful and just [true to His own nature and promises], and will forgive our sins and cleanse us continually from all unrighteousness [our wrongdoing, everything not in conformity with His will and purpose]."[29]

17. The Resurrection of The Body

"But if it is preached that Christ has been raised from the dead, how can some of you say that there is no resurrection of the dead? If there is no resurrection of the dead, then not even Christ has been raised. And if Christ has not been raised, our preaching is useless and so is your faith. More than that, we are then found to be false witnesses about God, for we have testified about God that he raised Christ from the dead. But he did not raise him if in fact the dead are not raised. For if the dead are not raised, then Christ has not been raised either. And if Christ has not been raised, your faith is futile; you are still in your sins. Then those also who have fallen asleep in Christ are lost. If only for this life we have hope in Christ, we are of all people most to be pitied. But Christ has indeed been raised from the dead, the first fruits of those who have fallen asleep."[30]

18. Life Everlasting

"I declare to you, brothers and sisters, that flesh and blood cannot inherit the kingdom of God, nor does the perishable inherit the imperishable. Listen, I tell you a mystery: We will not all sleep, but we will all be changed—in a flash, in the twinkling of an eye, at the last trumpet. For the trumpet will sound, the dead will be raised imperishable, and we will be changed. For the perishable must clothe itself with the imperishable, and the mortal with immortality.

When the perishable has been clothed with the imperishable, and the mortal with immortality, then the saying that is written will come true: 'Death has been swallowed up in victory.'

'Where, O death, is your victory? Where, O death, is your sting?'

The sting of death is sin, and the power of sin is the law. But thanks be to God! He gives us the victory through our Lord Jesus Christ. Therefore, my dear brothers and sisters, stand firm. Let nothing move you. Always give yourselves fully to the work of the Lord, because you know that your labor in the Lord is not in vain."[31]

"Most assuredly, I say to you, he who believes in Me has everlasting life."[32]

"For the wages of sin is death, but the free gift of God is eternal life in Christ Jesus our Lord."[33]

"The Apostles' Creed, though not written by the apostles, is the oldest creed of the Christian church and is the basis for others that followed. In its oldest form, the Apostles' Creed goes back to at least 140 A.D. Many of the early church leaders summed up their beliefs as they had an opportunity to stand for their faith—see, for example, 1 Timothy 6:12. These statements developed into a more standard form to express one's confession of faith at the time of baptism. It is not Scripture, but it is a simple list of the great doctrines of the faith. The word 'catholic' means "relating to the church universal" and was the word used in the original version of the Creed. It does not mean the Roman Catholic Church, but the church, the body of Christ, as a universal fellowship. The phrase, 'He descended into hell,' was not part of the creed in its earliest form."[37]

The process that God has for salvation is not complicated. Why would God make it impossible for all people to have eternal life in Him? He would not and did not. The eighteen essential points of the Apostles'

Creed, summarize the process in which salvation is guaranteed to those who believe and is a good summary of Christian doctrine. It should be seen as a seal for every believer's heart.

ACTIVATION

Read the Confession of Faith at the beginning of the chapter. Do you believe and receive this as truth? This is a great entry point to your salvation. If you would like to receive Jesus Christ as your savior and be welcomed into the kingdom of God please read the following prayer.

ACTIVATION PRAYER

Lord Jesus, I believe You are God's son and that You came into this earth to bring redemption and reconciliation. I believe you lived a sinless life and became sin for me. I believe You were wounded for my transgressions and bruised for my iniquities the chastisement of my peace was on You and by Your stripes I am healed.[35] I believe Your shed blood cleanses me from all my sins. I believe You gave Your life on the cross for me. I believe You were raised from the dead and are now seated at the right hand of the Father. I confess my sins and believe that I am forgiven. I ask that the Holy Spirit renew my spirit and declare that I am a new creature a new creation in You. Be my Savior reconciling me back to the Father. I ask You to be the Lord of my life. Amen.

CONCLUSION
God reveals, heals, and transforms

REVEAL

God reveals Himself to us in the process. He identifies who He is and who we are. To reveal is "to make known; disclose; divulge: to reveal a secret; to lay open to view; display; exhibit."[1] Moses was perfectly positioned for God to reveal Himself to him. His story is the story we heard in Sunday school as little children. A Hebrew baby who was placed in a basket, set adrift in the crocodile-infested Nile river, was caught in the tall grasses of the river, on banks of the daughter of Pharaoh. He found favor with the princess and was raised in the palace of Pharaoh, who taught him the Egyptian culture, mindset, gods, and traditions.

Moses had everything he could want, living as an Egyptian, but he did not know the one true God. His heart was softened by witnessing the harsh treatment of the Hebrews, and in his anger and attempt to defend a Hebrew, he killed a fellow Egyptian. Moses fled to Midian and was taken in by the Priest Jethro, who mentored him and gave him a wife. For forty years he lived there, learning yet another culture, language, customs, beliefs, trades and was introduced to God.

> "Now Moses was tending the flock of Jethro his father-in-law, the priest of Midian, and he led the flock to the far side of the wilderness and came to Horeb, the mountain of God. There the angel of the Lord appeared to him in flames of fire from within a bush. Moses saw that though the bush was on fire it did not burn up. So Moses thought, 'I will go over and see this strange sight—why the bush does not burn up.' When the Lord saw that he had gone over to look, God called to him from within the bush, 'Moses! Moses!' And Moses said, 'Here I am.'
>
> 'Do not come any closer,' God said. 'Take off your sandals, for the place where you are standing is holy ground.' Then he said, 'I am the God of your father the God of Abraham, the God of Isaac and the God of Jacob.' At this, Moses hid his face, because he was afraid to look at God."[2]

What an introduction! "The angel of the Lord appeared." God was intentional in getting Moses' attention. He used something so unusual that Moses had no choice but to stop and look at it. In the process, God will make sure He gets your attention. One of the most common worries that Christians have is whether or not they are hearing the voice of God. There is a concern that God will be speaking and they won't perceive it, leading to error. God knows it takes time for us to discover how He speaks to each of us. But He invites us daily to visit with Him so we can get familiar with Him. Moses responded to God's presence and voice by saying, "Here I am." God does not just talk to us without expecting us to respond. Our conversations with Him are two-way.

Then God showed Moses how to respond to His presence, "Take off your sandals, for the place where you are standing is holy ground." God is holy, and there is none above Him and none like Him. We must be reverent when we get in God's presence. This shows humility, honor, and respect. God began to describe Himself in the context of Moses' heritage. "I am the God of your Father, the God of Abraham, the God of Isaac, and the God of Jacob." It isn't clear if Moses knew who these people were based on the fact that he was raised an Egyptian, but I do believe God was teaching him about his heritage and that He was the God of those people who were suffering.

Moses had become a shepherd living in Midian. After the encounter with God, his situation and position did not change, but his perspective did. In the process, God will reveal Himself and important information about where you are that will change your perspective.

"The Lord said, 'I have indeed seen the misery of my people in Egypt. I have heard them crying out because of their slave drivers, and I am concerned about their suffering.'"[3] The information God revealed to Moses showed that God had the same heart for the Israelites that he did. He identified with them as "My people." This had to be an "ah-ha" moment for Moses, because he'd once had a heart for the same people. This was the God that the Hebrews worshiped. I'm sure he was familiar with some of their stories. God then tells Moses His plans: "So I have come down to rescue them from the hand of the Egyptians and to bring them up out of that land into a good spacious land, a land flowing with milk and honey."4

God has a plan for the process. He sees the whole picture, and understands the whole situation. He knows the whole story, and He is aware of every person represented. "So I said I will bring you up out of the suffering and oppression of Egypt to the land of the Canaanite, the Hittite, the Amorite, the Perizzite, the Hivite, and the Jebusite, to a land flowing with milk and honey."5

I believe if we look at the people and their practices in the land in Canaan, we can see that God had chosen the Israelites to be a people who would uphold certain moral standards so that the world would know that they can live with great blessing without compromising the character and holiness of God. The lifestyles of the Canaanite, the Hittite, the Amorite, the Perizzite, the Hivite, and the Jebusite, represented all that God hated. God did not hate the people but the way in which these groups of people treated others. God has so much more for humanity.

> "CANAANITES: This name means merchants who humiliate. They were financial giants. The Canaanites were motivated by greed and lust for the accumulation of earthly and material wealth.
>
> HITTITES: This name means terror. They were giants who brought fear, confusion and discouragement to others.
>
> AMORITES: They were people who were arrogant and boastful in their speech, who were always challenging. They had high self-esteem and this pride led to finding fault in others.

> PERIZZITES: They were people who had separated themselves and lived in unprotected villages without walls. They had no discipline and restrictions.
>
> HIVITES: They claimed to offer a good lifestyle, living by phrases such as 'if it feels good do it,' 'don't worry what other people think,' and 'look out for number one.' They lived a very luxurious life.
>
> JEBUSITES: They were people who exploited and polluted others through immoral activities."[6]
>
> "There are six things the LORD hates—no, seven things he detests: haughty eyes, a lying tongue, hands that kill the innocent, a heart that plots evil, feet that race to do wrong, a false witness who pours out lies, a person who sows discord in a family."[7]

The seven practices mentioned in the about scriptures are given to show that some behaviors and practices are detestable to God, and should be avoided. The groups of people mentioned display some of those "detestable" acts. Yet God still loved them and send His son to die for them.

> "'So now, go. I am sending you to Pharaoh to bring my people the Israelites out of Egypt.' But Moses, said to God, 'who am I that I should go to Pharaoh and bring the Israelites out of Egypt?'"[8]

In the process, God will always give you a task that you cannot do by yourself. There is a tall order you cannot fulfill without God's supervision and provision. "I will be with you. And this will be the sign to you that it is I who have sent you."[9] God is prepared and

the process

He has prepared you to get through the process. He did not ask Moses to go on his own, and He will not ask you to go on your own. Instead, God told Moses He would be with him and gave him a sign to confirm and comfort him. Look for the signs God has given you to confirm your purpose.

Throughout the rest of Exodus 3 and 4, God trains Moses to hear His voice and obey His command. He also explains the tools–the weapons He gives him, but most importantly God gives Moses His name, "I AM WHO I AM."[10] God is going to train you to hear His voice. He speaks to you like no other. God has given you tools and gifts to get the job done, and He will show you how to use them. But don't forget the most important part: God gave us His name, "I AM." The name God uses to describe Himself to Moses was very significate. "I AM," is all encompassing. God is self-existing, self-sufficient, self-caused, self-staining, complete and whoever you need Him to be right now in your current circumstance. Who do you need God to be today? A healer, a friend, a provider, a comforter, a deliverer, peace, joy, a place of safety? He is what you need every day and in every way.

HEAL

God brings healing during the process. It is not God's desire for us to be sick. Although there are many sicknesses and many have suffered and died from them, it is God who has compassion for us and wants us healed. However, the healing comes, it is important to know that God cares for you.

> "When Jesus heard what had happened, He withdrew by boat privately to a solitary place. Hearing of this, the crowds followed him on foot from the towns. When Jesus

landed and saw a large crowd, He had compassion on them and healed their sick."[11]

In this scripture, Jesus had just received news that his cousin John the Baptist was beheaded. He is mourning and wants to be alone to grieve. But the crowds are so desperate for healing and a touch from Him, that they follow Him. I believe there is such a desperation that they would have stayed all night, food or no food. Later in this chapter, Jesus feeds over 5000 people with two fish and five loaves of bread, truly miraculous. Jesus did not run from large crowds; he had compassion for them and healed their "sick."

How many people around the world do you think pray each day to Jesus? How many are asking for Jesus to heal them? How many are praying for lost kids, broken relationships, money for rent, drug-addicted family members, or safety for their deployed loved ones? Would you say it is more than a large crowd? The prayers of people around the world are filling the atmosphere continually. We are bombarding Jesus for answers to painful situations. Jesus knows, and as we read in the chapter called "Issues," Jesus was able to help them all. The healing process can touch us in places we thought would never get healed, using methods we would never suspect. Let's take some time to read some scriptures about healing:

- "He heals the brokenhearted and binds up their wounds."[12]
- "He restores my soul."[13]
- "Heal me, O Lord, and I will be healed; save me and I will be saved for you are the one I praise."[14]
- "He welcomed them and spoke to them about the kingdom of God and healed those who needed healing."[15]

- "But he was pierced for our transgressions, he was crushed for our iniquities;
- the punishment that brought us peace was on him, and by his wounds we are healed."[16]

TRANSFORM

To transform simply means to change. To change in form, appearance, structure, nature, character and behavior. The only way to change in any area of our lives is to reveal what is wrong, broken, or not suitable. Look at the steps of the process introduced in this book. God walks us through the process to reveal Himself and our need for Him. Though it takes time, the process is valuable. He wants to heal our wounds and issues, to help us unmask what we are hiding. He will transform our perspective on who we are and who is opposing us, so that we will be willing to change in areas of our lives and reflect God's character. "Do not be conformed to this world, but be transformed by the renewal of your mind, that by testing you may discern what is the will of God, what is good and acceptable and perfect."[17]

Often, we find it is hard to change our behavior about something if we cannot change the way we think about it. We do what we think. If you believe it is okay to lie, then you will continue to lie without giving it another thought. If you think it is acceptable to mistreat someone based on the color of their skin, then you will make a point to do it. The process for reformation and transformation can change a nation. The Civil Rights Movement reformed and transformed an entire culture, one day at a time, one nonviolent act at a time. Thousands of people paid the price for an opportunity to make history. Many were tortured, jailed, split from their families, lost their jobs and even murdered so this nation could change their perspective on the value of all life. This kind of reformation and transformation is still moving forward, even in 2017. But it happens by affecting one person, one family, one school, one community, one teacher, one church, one employer, one government official, and one court ruling at a time.

In the above scripture, the writer speaks of the "world" as the enemy. "Do not be conformed (in agreement with, bond to) the world."[18] The "world" in the passage is referencing the thought processes, customs, and traditions of our culture that oppose God and His commandments and character. True transformation is a complete change in one's mind, which is witnessed through one's actions: "to put off your old self, which belongs to your former manner of life and is corrupt through deceitful desires, and to be renewed in the spirit of your minds, and to put on the new self, created after the likeness of God in true righteousness and holiness."[19]

A transformed life in Christ can be summed up in this Bible passage, "His divine power has given us everything we need for a godly life… for if you do these things, you will never stumble, and you will receive a rich welcome into the eternal kingdom of our Lord and Savior Jesus Christ."[20]

Here are a few scriptures to read and pray about as you continue to transform:

- "Therefore, if anyone is in Christ, he is a new creation. The old has passed away; behold, the new has come."[21]

- "And I will give you a new heart, and a new spirit I will put within you. And I will remove the heart of stone from your flesh and give you a heart of flesh."[22]

- "And I am sure of this, that he who began a good work in you will bring it to completion at the day of Jesus Christ."[23]

- "For no good tree bears bad fruit, nor again does a bad tree bear good fruit, for each tree is known by its own fruit. For figs are not gathered from thorn bushes, nor are grapes picked from a bramble bush. The good person out of the good treasure of his heart produces good, and the evil person out of his evil treasure produces evil, for out of the abundance of the heart his mouth speaks."[24]

- "Search me, O God, and know my heart! Try me and know my thoughts! And see if there be any grievous way in me, and lead me in the way everlasting!"[25]

- "And they shall be my people, and I will be their God. I will give them one heart and one way, that they may fear me forever, for their own good and the good of their children after them. I will make with them an everlasting covenant, that I will not turn away from doing good to them. And I will put the fear of me in their hearts, that they may not turn from me."[26]

Every step of the process has a purpose, is valuable, and takes time; it requires us to unmask the hidden things. The process reveals the wounds of the soul. It can resolve issues and is designed to bring us into a place of victory. The enemy wants us paralyzed with rejection, fear, jealousy, and pride. He is always looking for a way to accuse us and trick us into partnering with him. God is the God of the angel armies and He is the Lord of the great heavenly host. The work of the cross through His son defeated every work of the enemy. We are no longer slaves; we are free to worship, live, bless, and grow.

conclusion

ACTIVATION

1. Reveal
Where are you in the process?
Is God revealing Himself to you for the first time?
Is God revealing His view of you?
Is God revealing a sin in your life that you need to repent of?
Is God revealing a new path, a new opportunity or a new assignment in your life?

2. Heal
Is there a need in your life for healing physically, emotionally, or relationally?
Have you been wounded in your soul, or do you suffer from a disease?
Is there trauma in your life because you or a loved one was abused?
Do you feel rejected by others?
Is there fear in your life?
Do you hide behind things or people?

3. Transform
Is God asking you to change your perspective on a situation or a group of people?
Has your heart been hardened because you won't receive the truth?
Is God challenging you to drop a specific habit that keeps you from growing closer to Him?

These can be tough questions for many of us. But the answer is easy and eternally sustainable—Jesus.

ACTIVATION PRAYER

Dear Lord, thank you for my time in the process. Thank you for revealing who You are in me and who I am in You. Thank you for healing my wounds and resolving issues in my life with great love and concern. Thank you for having compassion for me. Thank you that I can transform by the renewing of my mind in Christ Jesus. Thank you that I have the victory to overcome any and all hidden obstacles. Most of all thank you for sending your son to be the perfect sacrifice for my sins. I accept His sacrifice and look forward to spending each day with You.

about the author

Photo Credit: Sandra Aguilar Photography

Audra is a member of Patricia King's Women in Ministry Network (WIMN) and certified in Joan Hunter Ministries Healing School. She has been involved in women's ministry for over twenty years and has fulfilled many roles including worship leader, talk show host, women's ministry leader and spa owner.

Over the years, Audra has created curriculum for interactive Bible studies, developed ministry leadership teams and organized and hosted special events that assist in providing the atmosphere for God to transform women's lives. As a licensed esthetician, professional makeup artist, and wellness practitioner she teaches others the importance of taking care of themselves and leading a balanced life. She embraces each of these platforms to minister God's love and share biblical truths.

Audra is a "team-player leader," who challenges her peers to activate their gifts and move into position in the body of Christ. She is passionate about demonstrating godly character and leads by example. She teaches with wisdom and is transparent about her own successes and failures and always extends grace to those around.

Audra is the loving wife of Daryl Price, Jr. and mother of their five children. She understands and relates to women of diverse ethnic and generational backgrounds, and is a woman of influence, prayer warrior, prophetic activator, mentor and always sees the best in everyone she meets.

www.AudraPrice.com

endnotes

INTRODUCTION

1. Jeremiah 29:11 (NLT)
2. Psalm 23 (AMP)
3. "Through." *Dictionary.com*. www.dictionary.com/browse/through. Accessed 14 July 2017.
4. Isaiah 43:2 (NLT)
5. Deuteronomy 31:8 (NLT)
6. Psalm 37:23-24
7. Psalm 139:16
8. "Process." *Dictionary.com*. www.dictionary.com/browse/process. Accessed 14 July 2017.

CHAPTER 1

1. James 1:2-8
2. "Revelation." *Merriam-Webster.com* www.merriam-webster.com/dictionary/revelation. Accessed 27 June 2017.
3. "Knowledge." *Dictionary.com*. www.dictionary.com/browse/knowledge. Accessed 24 June 2017.
4. Deuteronomy 29:29
5. John 8:32 (NIV)
6. Amos 3:7
7. Romans 8:27
8. "Trial." *Dictionary.com*. www.dictionary.com/browse/trial. Accessed 14 July 2017.
9. "On trial" *Dictionary.com*. www.dictionary.com/browse/on--trial. Accessed 14 July 2017.

10. Hunt, June. "Trials." *Hope for the Heart.* www.hopefortheheart.org. Accessed 14 July 2017.

11. 1 Peter 4:12 (NLT)

12. Romans 5:3-5 (NLT)

13. 1 Peter 1:6 (NLT)

14. 1 Corinthians 10:13 (NLT)

15. 2 Corinthians 12:10 (NLT)

16. 2 Corinthians 12:9 (NLT)

17. "Due Course of Law." *Dictionary.com.* www.dictionary.com/browse/due-process-of-law. Accessed 22 April 2017.

18. Genesis 2:17 (KJV)

19. Acts 4:21 (NASB)

20. Deuteronomy 19:15 (KJV)

21. "Indictment." *YourDictionary.com*, n.d. Web. 21 November 2017. www.yourdictionary.com/Indictment.

22. John 18:29 (NASB)

23. Matthew 18:17

24. John 18:31 (KJV)

25. Romans 6:23

26. McCreary, Dann, "Biblical Due Process: God's Specification for Earthly Justice." flyinghouse.com/creator/theo/evidence.html. Accessed 27 June 2017.

27. Romans 11:1-2 (MSG)

28. Hebrews 11:2-3 (MSG)

29. Hebrews 11:2-3 (NLT)

30. Hebrews 11:4-16 (NLT)

31. Hebrews 11:32-35 (NLT)

32. Nehemiah 8:10

33. *Biblehub.com.* www.biblehub.com/greek/5046.htm. Accessed 5 June 2017.

34. "Wisdom." *Dictionary.com.* www.dictionary.com/browse/

wisdom Accessed 5 June 2017.

35. Proverbs 4:7
36. Proverbs 9:10
37. Proverbs 3:5-6
38. Malachi 3:2-3
39. Proverbs 18:10
40. Hunt, June. "God's Refining Process." *Hope for the Heart.* www.hopefortheheart.org/march-2015-gods-refining-process/ 31 August 2017.
41. Jeremiah 23:29 (NIV)
42. Proverbs 17:3 (NIV)
43. Proverbs 25:4 (NIV)
44. Psalm 12:6 (NIV)
45. Job 23:10 (NIV)
46. Genesis 1:27
47. 1 Peter 4:12-13
48. Malachi 3:3
49. Jeremiah 23:29
50. Galatians 5

CHAPTER 2

1. Hobar, Linda Lacour. *Mysteries of History.* Bright Ideas Press, 2010.
2. "How Stuff Works." health.howstuffworks.com/pregnancy-and-parenting/pregnancy/conception/conception-process2.htm. Accessed 6 June 2017.
3 "How Stuff Works." health.howstuffworks.com/pregnancy-and-parenting/pregnancy/conception/conception-process1.htm. Accessed 6 June 2017.
4. "How Stuff Works." health.howstuffworks.com/pregnancy-and-parenting/pregnancy/conception/conception-process2.htm.

Accessed 6 June 2017.

5. "How Stuff Works." health.howstuffworks.com/pregnancy-and-parenting/pregnancy/conception/conception-process3.htm. Accessed 6 June 2017.

6 "How Stuff Works." health.howstuffworks.com/pregnancy-and-parenting/pregnancy/conception/conception-process1.htm. Accessed 6 June 2017.

7. "Fetal Development." *Cleveland Clinic.org.* my.clevelandclinic.org/health/articles/fetal-development-stages-of-growth. Accessed 6 June 2017.

8. "Labor and Delivery." *Cleveland Clinic.org.* my.clevelandclinic.org/health/articles/labor-and-delivery. Accessed 6 June 2017.

9. "Pregnancy—Labor and Birth." *Department of Health and Human Services.* www.womenshealth.gov/pregnancy/childbirth-beyond/labor-birth.html. Accessed 6 June 2017.

10. Jeremiah 1:5 (NLT)

12. 1 Samuel 1:3-5

13. 1 Samuel 1:6

14. "Rival." *Dictionary.com.* www.dictionary.com/browse/rival. Accessed 6 June 2017.

15. 1 Peter 5:8

16. Revelation 12:10

17. 1 Samuel 1:7

18, 1 Samuel 1:8

19. 1 Samuel 1:9-10

20. 1 Samuel 1:9 (MSG)

21. 1 Samuel 1:11

22. 1 Samuel 1:12-14

23. 1 Samuel 1:15-16

24. 1 Samuel 1:17-18

25. 1 Samuel 1:19

26. 1 Samuel 1:20
27. 1 Samuel 1:21-28
28. 1 Samuel 3:1 (NASB)
29. "Deffinbaugh, Bob. "The Series: A Study of 1 Samuel." bible.org/seriespage/4-rise-samuel-and-fall-eli-and-sons-1-samuel-31-422. Accessed 6 June 2017.

CHAPTER 3

1. Genesis 1:26-27
2. Ephesians 1:4 (NLT)
3. "Image." *Dictionary.com*. www.dictionary.com/browse/image. Accessed 15 June 2017.
4. "Likeness." *Collins English Dictionary*. www.dictionary.com/browse/likeness. Accessed 15 June 2017.
5. "Attribute." *Dictionary.com*. www.dictionary.com/browse/attribute. Accessed 15 June 2017.
6. "Language." *Dictionary.com*. www.dictionary.com/browse/language. Accessed 15 June 2017.
7. Genesis 1:1-5 (NASB)
8. Genesis 1:26 (NASB)
9. John 1:1 (KJV)
10. Short, John Rendle. *The Image of God*. answersingenesis.org/who-is-god/creator-god/man-the-image-of-god/Man. Accessed 12 May 2017.
11. "Creativity." *Dictionary.com*. www.dictionary.com/browse/creativity. Accessed 15 June 2017.
12. "Love." *Dictionary.com*. www.dictionary.com/browse/love. Accessed 15 June 2017.
13. 1 John 4:7-8 (KJV)
14. Romans 5:8 (ESV)
15. Ephesians 25-29 (AMP)

16. "Holiness." *Dictionary.com*. www.dictionary.com/browse/holiness. Accessed 15 June 2017.

17. "Got Questions." www.gotquestions.org/holiness-Bible.html. Accessed 15 June 20117.

18. "Mercy." *Dictionary.com*. www.dictionary.com/browse/mercy. Accessed 6 July 2017.

19. Exodus 34:6-7 (ESV)

20. Ephesians 4:24; Colossians 3:10

21. Ham, Steve. "What is the Image of God? Image of God, Part 2." answersingenesis.org/genesis/what-is-image-of-god/ Accessed 6 July 2017.

22. 2 Corinthians 3:18 (NASB)

23. "Identity." *Online Etymology Dictionary*. www.dictionary.com/browse/identity. Accessed 15 June 2017.

24. Galatians 2:20 (NASB)

25. 2 Corinthians 5:17 (NASB)

26. Esther 1:1-12

27. Proverbs 31:30

28. Esther 2:1-4 (AMP)

29. "Harem." *Easy English Bible Dictionary*. www.easyenglish.bible/bible-dictionary/harem.htm Accessed 15 June 2017.

30. Esther 2:12-14

31. Kelley, Jack. "Esther's 12 Months of Beautification." gracethrufaith.com/ask-a-bible-teacher/esthers-12-months-of-beautification/. Accessed 15 June 2017.

32. Jones, Gary. "Honour Bound." www.scmp.com/magazines/post-magazine/article/1259246/honour-bound Accessed 16 Mar 2017.

33. Revelation 3:20 (MSG)

34. Psalm 139 (AMP)

35. Isaiah 49:1 (KJV)

36. Jeremiah 1:5 (KJV)

CHAPTER 4

1. "Mask." COBUILD *Advanced English Dictionary*. www.collinsdictionary.com/us/dictionary/english/mask. Accessed 22 May 2017.
2. Genesis 3:7-11 (NIV)
3. 2 Corinthians 5:21
4. 2 Corinthians 5:1-4 (NIV)
5. Exodus 32:25 (KJV)
6. Isaiah 47:3
7. Revelation 3:17 (KJV)
8. Revelation 16:15 (KJV)
9. Psalm 44:15 (NIV)
10. Jeremiah 8:12 (NIV)
11. Genesis 3:8-10 (NIV)
12. 2 Timothy 1:7
13. Ephesians 6:12
14. "False." *Dictionary.com*. www.dictionary.com/browse/false. Accessed 15 June 2017.
15. "Evidence." *Dictionary.com*. www.dictionary.com/browse/evidence. Accessed 15 June 2017.
16. "Appearing." *Dictionary.com*. www.dictionary.com/browse/appearing. Accessed 15 June 2017.
17. "Real." *Dictionary.com*. www.dictionary.com/browse/real. Accessed 15 June 2017.
18. Psalm 119:96 (NIV)
19. Genesis 4:8
20. Proverbs 6:34
21. Genesis 4:5,6
22. Song of Solomon 8:6
23. 1 Thessalonians 4:8
24. Genesis 4:5,6

25. Proverbs 13:10
26. Proverbs 14:30
27. Galatians 5:19
28. Proverbs 6:34 (NIV)
29. Proverbs 27.4 (NIV)
30. Galatians 5:22-23
31. 2 Corinthians 3:12-18

CHAPTER 5

1. Jeremiah 30:17 (NIV)
2. "Wound Care Centers." www.woundcarecenters.org/article/wound-therapies/vacuumassisted-closure. Accessed 16 Mar 2017.
3. Leaper DJ and Harding KG. *Wounds: Biology and Management.* www.clinimed.co.uk/wound-care/education/wound-essentials/phases-of-wound-healing.aspx. Accessed 16 Mar 2017.
4. Isaiah 53:5
5 Mark 10:27 (KJV)
6. Wittenberg, Adam. "How to Restore a Wounded Relationship." *Christian Living.* www.ihopkc.org/resources/blog/how-to-restore-a-wounded-relationship/ Accessed 16 Mar 2017.
7. Souza, Katie. Soul Decrees" 2nd Edition. Eleven Eleven Enterprises, 2015.
8. Psalm 41:4 (NASB)
9. Psalm 32:1-4 (AMP)
10. Psalm 32:5 (AMP0
11. Psalm 32:3-5 (MSG)
12. 2 Kings 1:29 (AKJS)
13. 2 Kings 4:18-21 (AMP)
14. 2 Kings 4:25-28 (AMP)
15. Deuteronomy 29:29
16. Hunter, Joan. *Freedom Beyond Comprehension.* Whitaker House,

2012.

17. "Self-Pity." *Dictionary.com.* www.dictionary.com/browse/self-pity. 27 June 2017.

18. Gagnon, Laura. *Healing the Heart of a Woman.* CreateSpace Independent Publishing Platform, 2016.

19. Leviticus 13:3

20. Leviticus 13:4

21. Leviticus 13:45-46

22. Leviticus 13:14-17

23. Mark 1:40-44

24. Gagnon, Laura. *Healing the Heart of a Woman.* CreateSpace Independent Publishing Platform, 2016.

25. 2 Chronicles 7:14

26. Luke 23:34

27. 1 Timothy 1:15, John 12:47, Colossians 1:14

28. John 19:30

CHAPTER 6

1. "Throng." *Dictionary.com.* www.dictionary.com/browse/throng. Accessed 6 June 2017.

2. "Got Questions." www.gotquestions.org/woman-issue-blood.html.Accessed 6 June 2017.

3. Leviticus 15:25-27

4. Mark 5:29-34

5. Mark 5:35

6. Mark 5:36

7. Mark 5:40

8. Mark 5:41-43

9. "Got Questions." www.gotquestions.org/Jairus-in-the-Bible.html Accessed 7 June 2017.

10. Matthew 9:27

11. Matthew 9:32
12. Luke 8:35-38

CHAPTER 7

1. Ezekiel 28:11-19 (MSG)
2. Isaiah 14:12-15
3. Luke 10:18
4. Revelation 9:1
5. 1 Peter 5:8
6. Revelation 12:10
7. Matthew 8:29; 2 Corinthians 11:3; 1 Peter 1:12
8. Luke 2:13; James 2:19; Revelation 12:17
9. Luke 8:28-31; 2 Timothy 2:26; Jude 6
10. Hebrews 1:14
11. "Got Questions. www.gotquestions.org/angels-Bible.html. Accessed 17 June 2017.
12. Psalm 24:7-10 (ESV)
13. Ephesians 6:10-13
14. Phillips, Ron. *Spiritual Warfare Bible*, called "The Army of Hell." Charisma House, 2012.
15. Ephesians 6:10-18 (NLT)
16. Ephesians 6:10-18 (MSG)
17. John 14:6
18. John 8:32
19. John 8:44
20. Proverbs 4:23
21. Isaiah 9:6
22. Hebrews 12:2
23. Philippians 2:5
24. 1 Corinthians 2:16
25. Psalm 48:11

26. Matthew 4:4
27. "Got Questions?" www.gotquestions.org/full-armor-of-God.html. Accessed 17 June 2017.
28. 1 Peter 5:8 (NIV)

CHAPTER 8

1. 2 Corinthians 10:3
2. "Stronghold." *Dictionary.com.* www.dictionary.com/browse/stronghold. 20 June 2017.
3. Daniels, Kimberly. *Clean House, Strong House: A Practical Guide to Understanding, Spiritual Warfare, Demonic Strongholds, and Deliverance.* Charisma House, 2003.
4. "Strong." *Dictionary.com.* www.dictionary.com/browse/strong. 20 June 2017.
5. "Hold." *Dictionary.com.* www.dictionary.com/browse/hold. 20 June 2017.
6. Luke 11:21-22
7. Matthew 12:29
8. Galatians 5:19-21
9. Luke 13:11
10. 2 Timothy 1:7
11. Acts 16:16-18
12. Hosea 4:12
13. Romans 8:15
14. Proverbs 16:18-19
15. Isaiah 19:14
16. 1 John 4:3
17. Isaiah 61:3
18. 1 John 4:6
19. Numbers 5:14
20. Romans 11:8

21. Mark 9:17-2
22. Leviticus 19:31
23. 1 Timothy 4:1
24. 1 John 4:6
25. Robeson, Drs. Jerry and Carol. *Strongman's His Name...What's His Game? An Authoritative Biblical Approach to Spiritual Warfare.* Whitaker House, 1983; Gagnon, Laura. *Healing the Heart of a Nation.* CreateSpace Independent Publishing Platform, 2016; *Spiritual Warfare Bible*, Charisma House, 2012. Phillips, Ron. "Twelve Root Strongholds." *Guide to Demons and Spiritual Warfare,* Charisma Media, 2010. 225-229.
26. "Reject." *Collins English Dictionary.* www.dictionary.com/browse/reject. Accessed 20 June 2017.
27. Galatians 5:22-23
28. Eckhardt, John. *Destroying the Spirit of Rejection.* Charisma House 2016.
29. Eckhardt, John. *Destroying the Spirit of Rejection.* Charisma House 2016. 44.
30. Eckhardt, John. *Destroying the Spirit of Rejection.* Charisma House 2016. 52.
31. Genesis 29:16-17
32. Genesis 29:18
33. Genesis 29:19-25
34. Genesis 29:26-30
35. "Rivalry in Polygamous Marriage: Part II." nabiesmagazin.blogspot.com/2012/08/rivalry-in-polygamous-marriage-part-ii.html. Accessed 20 June 2017.
36. Isaiah 53:3
37. John 1:11-12 (NIV)
38. Isaiah 53:4
39. Matthew 27:46

40. Isaiah 53:5 (NIV)
41. Hebrews 4:15-16 (ESV)
42. Psalm 111:10 (AMP)
43. 2 Timothy 1:7 (AMP)
44. 1 John 4:18
45. Eckhardt, John. *Destroying the Spirit of Rejection*. Charisma House 2016.
46. Helser, Jonathan David and Melissa. "No Longer Slaves." Bethel Music.
47. Proverbs 16:18-19
48. Eckhardt, John. *Destroying the Spirit of Rejection*. Charisma House, 2016. 92.
49. *Leviathan Exposed*. XP Ministries. www.xpministries.com/2016-leviathan-exposed/ Accessed 20 June 2017.
50. Hotchkin, Robert. *Leviathan Exposed*. XP Publishing, 2015. 30
51. Hotchkin, Robert. *Leviathan Exposed*. XP Publishing, 2015. 32-33
52. Hotchkin, Robert. *Leviathan Exposed*. XP Publishing, 2015. 35
53. Hotchkin, Robert. *Leviathan Exposed*. XP Publishing, 2015. 38-39
54. Job 41:1-10 (AMP)
55. James 4:6-7 (NLT)
56. Job 42:5-6 (AMP)
57. Acts 19:19-20
58. Job 42:5-6 (NIV)

CHAPTER 9

1. "Victim." *Dictionary.com*. www.dictionary.com/browse/victim. Accessed 29 June 2017.
2. "Victim Mentality." Wikipedia. en.wikipedia.org/wiki/Victim_mentality. Accessed 29 June 2017.

3. Lefkoe, Morty. *Do You Have 'Victim Mentality'? What to Do About It*, 18 December 2010. www.huffingtonpost.com/morty-lefkoe/victim-mentality_b_794628.html. Accessed 19 May 2017.
4 Romans 7:21 (NLT)
5 John 8:32 (NIV)
6. Roman 8:26-28 (NLT)
7. "Victorious." *Dictionary.com*. www.dictionary.com/browse/victorious. 29 June 2017.
8. Mattera, Joseph. *Daily Blog: Emotional Health*, 11 May 2017. josephmattera.org/20-contrasts-between-a-victim-and-victorious-mindset/. 29 June 2017.

CHAPTER 10

1. Zion Baptist Church, "Confession of Faith." Denver, Co.
2. Hebrews 11:6 (AMP)
3. 2 Corinthians 6:18 (NIV)
4. Genesis 1:1-2 (AMP)
5. John 3:16 (AMP)
6. Colossians 1:15 (AMP)
7. Philippians 2:9-11
8. Matthew 1:18-25 (AMP)
9. John 19:13-16 (NIV)
10. Matthew 27:50
11. Luke 23:46 (NIV)
12. John 19:28-30 (NIV)
13. Matt. 27.57-60 (NIV)
14. Mark 15:43-46 (NIV)
15. Luke 23:52-53 (NIV)
16. John 19:40-42 (NIV)
17. Matt. 28:1-6 (NIV)
18. Mark 16:1-6 (NIV)

19. Mark 16:19 (NIV)
20. Luke 24:50-51 (NIV)
21. Acts 1:6-11 (NIV)
22. Ephesians 1:19b-21 (NIV)
23. 2 Timothy 4:1 (NIV)
24. Matthew 28:19 (NIV)
25. Acts 1:4b-5 (NIV)
26. Galatians 5:22-23 (AMP)
27. George, Timothy. "What Do Protestant Churches Mean When They Recite 'I Believe in the Holy Catholic Church' and 'The Communion of Saints" in the Apostles' Creed?" www.christianitytoday.com/history/2008/september/what-do-protestant-churches-mean-when-they-recite-i.html. Accessed June 5, 2017.
28. Ephesians 4:1-6 (AMP)
29. 1 John 1:9 (AMP)
30. 1 Corinthians 15:12-20 (NIV)
31. 1 Corinthians 15:50-58 (NIV)
32. John 6:47
33. Romans 6:23 (NIV)
34. Graham, Billy. "What Is the Apostles' Creed?" *Answers by BGEA Staff.* June 1, 2004. billygraham.org/answer/what-is-the-apostles-creed. Accessed 24 June 2017.
35. Isaiah 53:5

CONCLUSION

1. "Reveal." *Dictionary.com.* www.dictionary.com/browse/reveal. 24 June 2017.
2. Genesis 3:1-6 (NIV)
3. Exodus 3:7 (NIV)
4. Exodus 3:8 (NIV)
5. Exodus 3:17 (AMP)

6. "The Seven Enemies of Israel in the Promised Land." *Bible Study Monthly.* July & August 2014. www.biblefellowshipunion.co.uk/2014/Sep_Oct/7Enemies.htm. Accessed 24 June 2017.

7. Proverbs 6:16-19 (NLT)

8. Exodus 3:10 (NIV)

9. Exodus 3:12 (NIV)

10. Exodus 3:14 (NIV)

11. Matt. 14:13-14 (NIV)

12. Psalm 147:3 (NIV)

13. Psalm 23:3 (NIV)

14. Jeremiah 17:14 (NIV)

15. Luke. 9:11 (NIV)

16. Isaiah 53:5 (NIV)

17. Romans 12:2 (ESV)

18. Romans 12:2 (AMP)

19. Ephesians 4:22-24 (ESV)

20. 2 Peter 1:3, 8 (NIV)

21. 2 Corinthians 5:17 (ESV)

22. Ezekiel 36:26 (ESV)

23. Philippians 1:6 (ESV)

24. Luke 6:43-45

25. Psalm 139:23-24

26. Jeremiah 32:38-40 (ESV)

works cited

"Appearing." *Dictionary.com*. www.dictionary.com/browse/appearing. Accessed 15 June 2017.

"Attribute." *Dictionary.com*. www.dictionary.com/browse/attribute. Accessed 15 June 2017.

The Bible. The Amplified Version. *Biblehub.com*. Biblehub, 2016. biblehub.com. Accessed 24 June 2017.

The Bible. The English Standard Version. *Biblehub.com*. Biblehub, 2016. biblehub.com. Accessed 24 June 2017.

The Bible. The Message. *Biblehub.com*. Biblehub, 2016. biblehub.com. Accessed 24 June 2017.

The Bible. New American Standard Version. *Biblehub.com*. Biblehub, 2016. biblehub.com. Accessed 24 June 2017.

The Bible. New Heart English Bible. *Biblehub.com*. Biblehub, 2016. biblehub.com. Accessed 24 June 2017.

The Bible. New International Version. *Biblehub.com*. Biblehub, 2016. biblehub.com. Accessed 24 June 2017.

The Bible. New King James Version. *Biblehub.com*. Biblehub, 2016. biblehub.com. Accessed 24 June 2017.

The Bible. The New Living Translation. *Biblehub.com*. Biblehub, 2016. biblehub.com. Accessed 24 June 2017.

"Creativity." *Dictionary.com*. www.dictionary.com/browse/creativity. Accessed 15 June 2017.

Daniels, Kimberly. *Clean House, Strong House: A Practical Guide to Understanding, Spiritual Warfare, Demonic Strongholds, and Deliverance.* Charisma House, 2003.

Deffinbaugh, Bob. "The Series: A Study of 1 Samuel." bible.org/seriespage/4-rise-samuel-and-fall-eli-and-sons-1-samuel-31-422. Accessed 6 June 2017.

"*Due Course of Law.*" *Dictionary.com.* www.dictionary.com/browse/due-process-of-law. Accessed 27 April 2017.

Eckhardt, John. *Destroying the Spirit of Rejection.* Charisma House 2016.

"Evidence." *Dictionary.com* www.dictionary.com/browse/evidence. Accessed 15 June 2017.

"False." *Dictionary.com.* www.dictionary.com/browse/false. Accessed 15 June 2017.

"Fetal Development." *Cleveland Clinic.org.* my.clevelandclinic.org/health/articles/fetal-development-stages-of-growth. Accessed 6 June 2017.

Gagnon, Laura. *Healing the Heart of a Woman.* CreateSpace Independent Publishing Platform, 2016.

Gagnon, Laura. Healing the Heart of a Nation. CreateSpace Independent Publishing Platform, 2016., 2016,

George, Timothy. "What Do Protestant Churches Mean When They Recite 'I Believe in the Holy Catholic Church' and 'The Communion of Saints" in the Apostles' Creed?" www.christianitytoday.com/history/2008/september/what-do-protestant-churches-mean-when-they-recite-i.html. Retrieved June 5, 2017.

"Got Questions." www.gotquestions.org/angels-Bible.html. Accessed 17 June 2017.

"Got Questions?" www.gotquestions.org/full-armor-of-God.html Accessed 17 June 2017.

"Got Questions." www.gotquestions.org/holiness-Bible.html. Accessed 15 June 2017.

"Got Questions." www.gotquestions.org/Jairus-in-the-Bible.html Accessed 7 June 2017.

"Got Questions." www.gotquestions.org/woman-issue-blood.html. Accessed 6 June 2017.

Graham, Billy. "What Is the Apostles' Creed?" *Answers by BGEA Staff.* June 1, 2004. billygraham.org/answer/what-is-the-apostles-creed. Accessed 24 June 2017.

Ham, Steve. "What is the Image of God? Image of God, Part 2." answersingenesis.org/genesis/what-is-image-of-god/ Accessed 6 July 2017.

"Harem." *Easy English Bible Dictionary.* www.easyenglish.bible/bible-dictionary/harem.htm Accessed 15 June 2017.

Healing for the Soul. Wrong source, see June Hunt, Forgiveness

Helser, Jonathan David and Melissa. "No Longer Slaves." Bethel Music.

Hobar, Linda Lacour. *Mysteries of History.* Bright Ideas Press, 2010.

"Hold." *Dictionary.com.* www.dictionary.com/browse/hold. 20 June 2017.

"Holiness." *Dictionary.com.* www.dictionary.com/browse/holiness. Accessed 15 June 2017.

Hotchkin, Robert. *Leviathan Exposed.* XP Publishing, 2015

"How Stuff Works." health.howstuffworks.com/pregnancy-and-parenting/pregnancy/conception/conception-process2.htm. Accessed 6 June 2017.

"How Stuff Works." health.howstuffworks.com/pregnancy-and-parenting/pregnancy/conception/conception-process1.htm. Accessed 6 June 2017.

"How Stuff Works." health.howstuffworks.com/pregnancy-and-parenting/pregnancy/conception/conception-process2.htm. Accessed 6 June 2017.

"How Stuff Works." health.howstuffworks.com/pregnancy-and-parenting/pregnancy/conception/conception-process3.htm. Accessed 6 June 2017.

"How Stuff Works." health.howstuffworks.com/pregnancy-and-parenting/pregnancy/conception/conception-process1.htm. Accessed 6 June 2017.

Hunt, June. "God's Refining Process." *Hope for the Heart.* www.hopefortheheart.org/march-2015-gods-refining-process/ 31 August 2017

Hunt, June. "Trials." *Hope for the Heart.* www.hopefortheheart.org. Accessed 14 July 2017.

Hunter, Joan. *Freedom Beyond Comprehension.* Whitaker House, 2012.

"Identity." *Online Etymology Dictionary*. www.dictionary.com/browse/identity. Accessed 15 June 2017.

"Image." *Dictionary.com*. www.dictionary.com/browse/image. Accessed 15 June 2017.

"Inner Healing 101: Healing Emotional Wounds." www.greatbiblestudy.com/inner_healing_101.php. Accessed 16 Mar 2017.

Jones, Gary. "Honour Bound." www.scmp.com/magazines/post-magazine/article/1259246/honour-bound. Accessed 16 Mar 2017.

Kelley, Jack. "Esther's 12 Months of Beautification." gracethrufaith.com/ask-a-bible-teacher/esthers-12-months-of-beautification/ Accessed 15 June 2017.

"Knowledge." *Dictionary.com*. www.dictionary.com/browse/knowledge. Accessed 24 June 2017.

"Labor and Delivery." *Cleveland Clinic.org*. my.clevelandclinic.org/health/articles/labor-and-delivery. Accessed 6 June 2017.

"Language." *Dictionary.com*. www.dictionary.com/browse/language. Accessed 15 June 2017.

Lefkoe, Morty. *Do You Have 'Victim Mentality'? What to Do About It*, 18 December 2010. www.huffingtonpost.com/morty-lefkoe/victim-mentality_b_794628.html. Accessed 19 May 2017.

Leviathan Exposed. XP Ministries. www.xpministries.com/2016-leviathan-exposed/ Accessed 20 June 2017.

"Likeness." *Collins English Dictionary.* www.dictionary.com/browse/likeness. Accessed 15 June 2017.

"Love." *Dictionary.com.* www.dictionary.com/browse/love. Accessed 15 June 2017.

"Mask." *COBUILD Advanced English Dictionary.* www.collinsdictionary.com/us/dictionary/english/mask. Accessed 22 May 2017.

Mattera, Joseph. *Daily Blog: Emotional Health.* 11 May 2017. josephmattera.org/20-contrasts-between-a-victim-and-victorious-mindset/ 29 June 2017.

McCreary, Dann, "Biblical Due Process: God's Specification for Earthly Justice." flyinghouse.com/creator/theo/evidence.html. Accessed 27 June 2017.

"Mercy." *Dictionary.com.* www.dictionary.com/browse/mercy. Accessed 6 July 2017.

"The Miracles of Jesus." bible.org/seriespage/8-cleansing-leper. Accessed 15 June 2017.

"On trial" *Dictionary.com.* www.dictionary.com/browse/on--trial. Accessed 14 July 2017.

Phillips, Ron. Phillips, Ron. Spiritual Warfare Bible Spiritual Warfare Bible, called "The Army of Hell." Charisma House

Phillips, Ron. *Everyone's Guide to Demons and Spiritual Warfare.* Charisma House, 2010. 86-87 and 225-229

"Pregnancy—Labor and Birth." *Department of Health and Human Services.* www.womenshealth.gov/pregnancy/childbirth-beyond/labor-birth.html. Accessed 6 June 2017.

"Process." *Dictionary.com.* www.dictionary.com/browse/process. Accessed 14 July 2017.

"Real." *Dictionary.com.* www.dictionary.com/browse/real. Accessed 15 June 2017.

"Reject." *Collins English Dictionary.* www.dictionary.com/browse/reject. Accessed 20 June 2017.

"Reveal." *Dictionary.com.* www.dictionary.com/browse/reveal. 24 June 2017.

"Revelation." *Merriam-Webster.com.* www.merriam-webster.com/dictionary/revelation. Accessed 27 June 2017.

"Rival." *Dictionary.com.* www.dictionary.com/browse/rival. Accessed 6 June 2017.

"Rivalry in Polygamous Marriage: Part II." nabiesmagazin.blogspot.com/2012/08/rivalry-in-polygamous-marriage-part-ii.html. Accessed 20 June 2017.

Robeson, Drs. Jerry and Carol. *Strongman's His Name.. What's His Game? An Authoritative Biblical Approach to Spiritual Warfare.* Whitaker House, 1983.

"Self-Pity." *Dictionary.com.* www.dictionary.com/browse/self-pity. 27 June 2017.

"The Seven Enemies of Israel in the Promised Land." *Bible Study Monthly.* July & August 2014. www.biblefellowshipunion.co.uk/2014/Sep_Oct/7Enemies.htm. Accessed 24 June 2017.

Short, John Rendle. *The Image of God.* answersingenesis.org/who-is-god/creator-god/man-the-image-of-god/Man. Accessed 12 May 2017.

"Strong." *Dictionary.com.* www.dictionary.com/browse/strong. 20 June 2017.

"Stronghold." *Dictionary.com*. www.dictionary.com/browse/stronghold. 20 June 2017.

Souza, Katie. "Healing Your Soul: Real Keys to the Miraculous." Uploaded by Stashagarcia101. 7 February 2015. www.youtube.com/watch?v=rCV-O4ZGXOE.

"Throng." *Dictionary.com*. www.dictionary.com/browse/throng. Accessed 6 June 2017.

"Through." *Dictionary.com*. www.dictionary.com/browse/through. Accessed 14 July 2017 "Through."

"Trial." *Dictionary.com*. www.dictionary.com/browse/trial. Accessed 14 July 2017.

"Victim." *Dictionary.com*. www.dictionary.com/browse/victim. Accessed 29 June 2017.

"Victim Mentality." Wikipedia. en.wikipedia.org/wiki/Victim_mentality. Accessed 29 June 2017.

"Victorious." *Dictionary.com*. www.dictionary.com/browse/victorious. 29 June 2017.

"What Does the Bible Say About Transformation?" *Gotquestions.org*. www.gotquestions.org/Bible-transformation.html. Gotquestions.org. Accessed 24 June 2017.

Wittenberg, Adam. "How to Restore a Wounded Relationship." *Christian Living*. www.ihopkc.org/resources/blog/how-to-restore-a-wounded-relationship/ Accessed 16 Mar 2017.

"Wound Care Centers." www.woundcarecenters.org/article/wound-therapies/vacuumassisted-closure. Accessed 16 Mar 2017.

Zion Baptist Church, "Confession of Faith." Denver, Co.

All Bible verses are taken from the New King James Version of the Bible unless otherwise noted.